W.C. Bryant in Roslyn

BY
DIANE TARLETON
BENNETT
AND
LINDA TARLETON

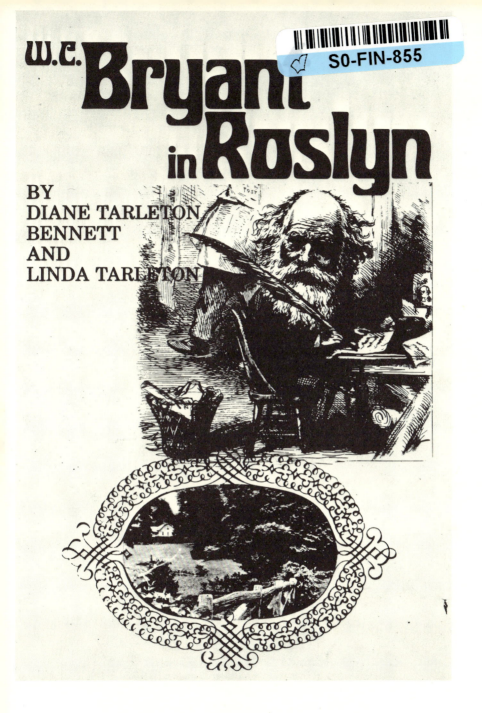

PUBLISHED BY THE BRYANT LIBRARY
ROSLYN, LONG ISLAND, NEW YORK
1978

DEDICATION

To our father, Owen Hill Tarleton, (May 29, 1898 to December 6, 1977) who read us "Thanatopsis" and *The Rubaiyat* in lieu of bedtime stories, and then told us marvelous ones of his own devising. Having no sons, he urged his four daughters on to careers, and then advised those of us who chose writing that he had never read a book written by a woman. He's been spared the duty of reading this one, but it is for him still—undertaken in love and an awareness of the continuity of life which he imparted to us—a sense he shared with Bryant.

ACKNOWLEDGEMENTS

It's said that writers are lucky to average 10 good pages of copy a day. We were sometimes surprised, in the turmoil and trauma of writing this book, to average 10 good words a day on paper, or to get even one friendly word from our families.

The list of those "without whom"—is a long one:

Altha Cook Tarleton, our mother, who not only supported us in our work on the book, but even read it;

John Bruno, exceedingly patient and loving spouse of Linda Tarleton-Bruno;

Elizabeth Bennett, who devoted long hours, shoe leather, and incisive thinking to her peripatetic research efforts.

Nancy Silverman, constant encourager, friend, and prodder, and *Irving Silverman,* infinitely patient supporter;

Evelyn Philips, eagle eye, dear friend, severe critic;

Roy Moger, Roslyn village historian, author of *Roslyn, Then and Now,* who kindly read the book in manuscript and whose own book was so helpful to us;

Michael D'Innocenzio, Hofstra University professor, who read the manuscript while he was in the midst of preparing a conference at the university about Bryant;

Sharyn Deutsch, for diligent research efforts and insightful comments;

Dorothy King, curator of the Long Island Collection at East Hampton Library; *Paul Rubin,* curator, New York Public Library Bryant Collection; and *Richard Winche,* and *Mary Louise Matera,* curators, Nassau County Museum, who all were unfailingly helpful in assuring accessibility to private and public collections and material;

Walter Donald Kring, author of a two-volume history of All Souls Church in New York City, where Bryant was a parishioner. Mr. Kring, minister of All Souls, went beyond generosity by sending us not only a copy of the published first volume but applicable portions of his unpublished manuscript of the second volume, and in addition answered many questions.

The Reverend Arthur Cullen Bryant, pastor of St. James Lutheran Church of Vandalia, Illinois, for his good suggestions and his kindness, and *the staff of the Bryant Library* for their willing help throughout the year of this project;

The Roslyn Savings Bank, for its continuing support of the Bryant Library's projects during the centennial year of 1978.

Not least of our thank-you's goes to *Theodore M. Black,* president, Walter J. Black, Inc., Flower Hill, Roslyn, New York, for his generous support of the library project.

CONTENTS

AUTHORS' PREFACE

Once William Cullen Bryant wrote some few pages of autobiographical material, saying as he began that he would abandon the project if he decided that he had nothing of interest to relate, as more famous men might have. He also said he had not the memory for dates and the recall of incidents that would be needed for an autobiography.

He did abandon the project. It remained for succeeding biographers to take it up, among them his son-in-law, Parke Godwin, as well as numerous others, including Tremaine McDowell, Allan Nevins and Charles Brown.

This book relies on those works and more, but has no claim to the status of biography. The Bryant Library's conception of the book, and our purpose in writing it, had its origins in Bryant's long residence in Roslyn, and the fact that it was his intent, in a plan executed by his daughter Julia after his death in 1878, to give the library, subsequently named after him, to the village of Roslyn. The book explores the 35 years that Bryant spent here, gives an overview of his life and tries to demonstrate the complexity and the strengths of a man who had a signal effect on his time—the first years of the republic of the United States—and who has been singularly neglected by history. This despite the fact that Bryant, who was born during the Presidency of Washington and died during Hayes' administration, was a radical journalist whose influence on his era was greater than he could ever have imagined.

Because the authors also believe that Bryant's poetry has been too much denigrated by a succession of critics, there is a section in the book that probes and evaluates the work that he perceived to be his most joyful occupation. In all, we hope to show the man of whom the Reverend Dr. Mark Hopkins, ex-president of Williams College (Bryant's alma mater) said that he had "the wisdom of age in his youth, and the fire of youth in his age."

Diane Tarleton Bennett
Mineola, New York
Linda Tarleton
Port Washington, New York
December, 1978

A TRIBUTE TO BRYANT

The written word is the most potent tool ever devised by the intellect of man in his short possession of the universe—potent because it effected continuity without his presence. Now history could be transmitted without being entrusted to the vagaries of memory.

Thus a book about William Cullen Bryant seems a fitting centennial tribute to the man who passionately loved books his life long, collecting them by judicious selection and reading and rereading his eclectic choices. His books were not showy boastings—they were loved companions.

This project for the 100th anniversary of his death recognizes too Bryant's desire to share his love for books with the community he adopted as his home, where he spent the last 35 years of his life in joyous communion with nature. We believe this to be the first such venture ever commissioned by a library, and it is an undertaking we think Bryant would have approved, though he surely would have been somewhat embarrassed by the attention, since he refused even to have the library at Roslyn named after him. We hope the book will add to the understanding of later generations of Roslynites about the man who gave a whole village the valued gift of the written word in all its power and variety.

December, 1978

THE LIBRARY

Bryant's monument in Roslyn is the library he gave: he attempted to make light of his gift by saying he wanted to donate a library because "the people have no places to meet in the evening save barrooms." But it was a serious gift, and one that he firmly believed would be of lasting value.

The reading room and lecture hall grew over the years from a small structure to a full-fledged library with his son-in-law, Parke Godwin, as its first president. Membership dues helped offset the costs of running it, though there were times when Bryant might have been pained at the difficulties the library faced—the year in which not one reader paid the required fee for home borrowing, or another when only 14 persons took out books. But the library survived those first years, and subsequent successful years more than compensated for them. Bryant surely would be pleased if he could revisit now and see the burgeoning results of his gift.

A burning sky
is o'er me,
The sands beneath me
glow,
As onward,
onward, wearily,
In the sultry morn I go

DREAMS AND PROMISES

IT WAS a long progress for William Cullen Bryant from his birth in Cummington, Massachusetts, in 1794, to Manhattan and Roslyn, and an adulthood that saw the fulfillment of many long held dreams and promises.

Poet, lawyer, newspaper editor, horticulturist, linguist, world traveler, radical champion of the common man in a time of general insensitivity to basic human needs, William Cullen Bryant was a dominant figure in the literary and political life of the 19th century. He lived in a seminal time for both the United States and New York, the state he adopted as his home.

9

Remembered in American literature as a nature poet, and sometimes called the first American voice in poetry, he is too complex and diverse a man to be recalled in so limited a way. His story is the story of 19th century America, iconoclastic, vibrant, vital, and moving from a rural agricultural economy to an urban-centered, industrial society. His fortunes grew with the century, and so did his interests. It is a measure of the man that he could separate so completely his places of work and leisure, hedging himself in wherever he lived, with gardens as barriers against his places of workaday toil. He adopted a social manner, too, that proved a barrier against intrusion—one that led acquaintances to believe him cold.

He was meticulous in all he did. Bryant's goals were never empty promises; they were designed for fulfillment. He devoted the same passionate energy to planting a tree as he did to writing an editorial defending the rights of workers to strike or to finding the perfect word in rewriting a poem. His goals always became tangible examples of his talent, and his fluidity and flexibility of mind enabled him to rise above popular stances to assert, from a position of authority achieved through diligence and talent, views that were ethical, though radical and controversial. It was that quality which earned him the respect of his contemporaries. After his death, his journalistic contributions were all but forgotten, and his reputation as a poet declined. Perhaps never before has a poet been so feted and honored in his lifetime, and so savagely attacked after his death.

Even Van Wyck Brooks, who appraised Bryant fully as a man who stood above the "spawn of Byronism", Homeric in his total accomplishments (an allusion to the man's diverse interests and epic goals as much as to his translations of Homer's works), also savaged his poetry, calling it "a palsied gift." But in fairness to the poet, if "Thanatopsis" and "Mutation" were all that he had written, he would have needed to make no apologia for his poetic gift. Poetry was his first life choice. He was encouraged to write by his father, Dr. Peter Bryant, a surgeon and classical scholar who had himself published some poems. Bryant at 13 years penned a long poem attacking Thomas Jefferson. The work's point of view was in keeping with his father's politics, but by his mature years Bryant changed so dramatically that he dissociated himself from the childish effort that had been published and widely circulated in pamphlet form, through his father's efforts.

He continued to write, with his father as his mentor, editor, and harshest critic. In a letter to Bryant's mother, Sarah Snell Bryant, his father once wrote that their son later would be ashamed of those first efforts. While that was a prophetic, or an understandably trenchant observation, it did not stop Dr. Bryant from urging his son on to greater effort and energy.

Bryant, the second child of Peter and Sarah Bryant, grew up in a home notable in Cummington for its extensive library of English, Greek and Latin literature. He early grew accustomed to books as companions as well as sources of ideas, knowledge and stimulation.

He read Cowper and Southey, Burns and Pope (whom his mother had once called "the libeler of her sex" for his essay "Epistle on the Character of Women"). In the young nation, no indigenous body of literature had been developed, save for the patriotic and rhetorical writings of the hewers of the new country's shape and form. For this reason, a literary education relied heavily on the authors of the mother country as well as others, and Bryant was steeped in those cultures. He was perhaps lucky, in this period of his life, in his position in the family, for his parents, as yet unworn by the burdens of family expenses, encouraged his studies.

Though the date is disputed by scholars, Bryant is credited with penning one of his best-known poems, "Thanatopsis," in 1811, at the age of 17. Whether it was written then, or one or two years later is of little moment in the long view, since the work stands as one of the first and most important in the literature of the new country. Of all his work, it is still the one most often quoted.

His long progress through those childhood years to pre-eminence in his time as journalist and man of letters included schooling at Williams College in Williamstown, Massachusetts, and a short, unhappy career as a lawyer. It was an occupation that at first he would not have dreamed of trying, despite his aptitude for logic later evidenced in his incisive editorials for The New York Evening Post.

Because of some financial reverses suffered by his father, young Bryant and his brothers and sisters grew up in the home of his maternal grandfather, Ebenezer Snell, a man whose forbidding, traditional religion was his life. It was under the tutelege of this grim magistrate that Bryant absorbed the virtues of early American life, where the work ethic was paramount and pleasure a matter for Calvinistic condemnation.

Bryant's childhood was one of many illnesses, and much hard farm work, apart from his studies. Still, for all the hardships, it was at Cummington that he learned a pleasure that was a lifelong source of delight to him; his daily long tramps through the woods and fields.

He was only 16 when he entered Williams College at the sophomore level. He found the work unchallenging, the restrictions on the students burdensome, and did not participate with any fervor in student activities. When one of his friends, Charles Avery, decided to attend Yale, Bryant was intrigued by the thought, and wrote to his father seeking permission to continue his studies there. But that proved impossible. Dr. Bryant was forced to tell his son that financial difficulties and the needs of the rest of his children meant that the costs of a Yale education were beyond their means. Bryant was despondent when he learned the news, but he adapted well enough. After casting about for an alternative, he chose law as a career that would earn him a living. He had been bitterly unhappy at the loss of the dream of literature as a vocation but he overcame his pain and, following 11 the custom of the time, began "reading law" in an attorney's office in preparation for admission to the bar.

He moved to Worthington, a scant distance from his Cummington home, to study with Samuel Howe, a friend of his father. Bryant gave his new profession the same strong attention that he was to maintain as a work attitude his life long. If he adopted the law with some sour grapes avidity, nonetheless his compulsion to succeed would not permit anything less than his best effort.

Bryant was writing poetry, and wrestling with his desire to devote himself to literature, while he studied with Howe. Still an adolescent, filled with the longings, fears and loves of youth, he was imitative and florid, writing poetry during this period that was gloomy and fearful of death. But at the same time he was working assiduously to complete his studies with Howe, who frowned on Bryant's attention to such unproductive vagaries. In 1814, having finished his apprentice studies, he moved on to Bridgewater, Massachusetts, for office training in the law under attorney (and Congressman) William Baylies. He continued meanwhile to write, even though his studies and the duties of his job grew ever more demanding—perhaps, as biographer Charles Brown notes—because Congressman Baylies was so often in Washington and Bryant was left in charge of the office.

Bryant tried in vain during the War of 1812 with England to obtain a lieutenancy in the army that Massachusetts was raising for its protection, offering his services to Governor Caleb Strong. He had a second motive in this; he knew that he was provincial and hoped to polish his rustic ways through army service. But in 1814, the year before he was admitted to law practice by a bar committee, he became ill with symptoms of consumption (possibly a tubercular complaint). He had to go home to Cummington to recover. It wasn't until 1816 that he attained the commission he sought.

Bryant was not quite 21 when he obtained his license to practice law. After a short sojourn to recover at his parent's home, he moved to Plainfield, Massachusetts, where he set up an office. That decision resulted in a short-lived and unhappy stay; it was a small town and far from lively enough to suit the young man. When George Ives, a young attorney in Great Barrington, suggested they set up in partnership together, he accepted with alacrity, and was soon established in his new office. Within a year he had bought out Ives's interest, and despite various lapses into dissatisfaction because of his preference for a literary life, worked hard at his new career.

Even so, it was obvious then that Bryant would not embrace the law with the same fervor with which he might have embraced a literary career. In a letter to William Baylies in 1817 he wrote: "You ask whether I am pleased with my profession. Alas, Sir, the Muse was my first love and the remains of that passion which, not rooted out nor yet chilled into extinction, will always, I fear, cause me to look coldly at the severe beauties of Themis. Yet

12

I tame myself to its labours as well as I can and have endeavored to discharge with punctuality and attention such of the duties of my profession as I was capable of performing."

It was at this time that Bryant also wrote the lines that defined his scorn for his legal labors and the desire for a more contemplative life which ultimately led him to abandon the legal profession.

"Though forced to drudge for the dregs of men,
And scrawl strange words with the barbarous pen,
And mingle among the jostling crowd,
Where the sons of strife are subtle and loud—
I often come to this quiet place,
To breathe the airs that ruffle thy face,
And gaze upon thee in silent dream,
For in thy lonely and lovely stream
An image of that calm life appears
That won my heart in my greener years."

But it was also the period when he wrote "O Fairest of the Rural Maids," the time when romance entered his life in the person of Frances Fairchild. Despite Bryant's gentle boasting about his romances in letters to friends, his deeper feelings were not touched until he met Frances. Frances, called Fanny, whom he met at a social gathering in Great Barrington, was 19 when he first saw her. Small and dainty, with long brown hair and grey eyes, she captivated Bryant. Her parents had died of a fever and she had come to live with a sister and brother-in-law, Mr. and Mrs. Allan Henderson. Over the next few months, Bryant wrote her many letters, which he never sent. They were alternately playful and serious in tone, but all of them were designed to encourage her to consider him as the tender, devoted suitor he was. He also praised her virtues in a number of unpublished poems, in addition to a familiar published poem, the mannered and romantic "O Fairest of the Rural Maids." He courted her with persistence, and they were married formally in the home of Frances's sister, on January 11, 1821. But first they pledged their intentions and their love in a contract that dedicated their lives to each other "here and hereafter." The contract, sealing an abiding love that spanned 45 years until Fanny's death in 1861, read:

"May almighty God mercifully take care of our happiness here and hereafter. May we ever continue constant to each other, and mindful of our mutual promises of attachment and truth. In due time, if it be the will of Providence, may we become more nearly connected with each other, and together may we lead a long, happy and innocent life, without any diminution of affection, till we die. May there never be any jealousy, distrust, coldness or dissatisfaction between us—nor occasion for any—nothing but kindness, forbearance, mutual confidence, and attention to each other's happiness. And that we may be less unworthy of so great a blessing, may we be assisted to cultivate all the benign and charitable affections and offices not only toward each other, but toward our neighbors, the human race, and all the creatures of God. 13

And in all things wherein we have done ill, may we properly repent our error, and may God forgive us and dispose us to do better. When at last we are called to render back the life we have received, may our deaths be peaceful, and may God take us to his bosom."

Bryant traditionally reserved such tender expressions for his poetry, and in letters to his family was inclined to write either drolly or matter-of-factly. He was, however, an inveterate correspondent, who throughout a long life kept up running commentaries—some 2,500 letters—with friends, relatives, acquaintances and business contacts. He did not let his new status as a married man go unheralded in print. In a half-mocking letter to his mother and brothers and sisters, he announced the event. Interpreted by some as too flippant a description of an occasion which called for more seriousness and joy, it said in part: "The gentleman . . . then muttered certain cabalistical expressions which I was much too frightened to remember, but I recollect that at the conclusion I was given to understand that I was married to a young lady of the name of Frances Fairchild, whom I perceived standing by my side, and I hope in the course of a few months to have the pleasure of introducing to you as your daughter-in-law, which is a matter of some interest to the poor girl, who has neither father nor mother in the world . . ."

It has been Bryant's lot to be interpreted by his contemporaries, and then reinterpreted by new generations of writers, as a humorless, cold, and arrogant man, and then to be criticized besides for being playful at inappropriate times. But the seriousness of the marriage vows that Fanny and Bryant took in writing, before their formal marriage in 1821, ought to offset the criticism of that letter announcing his marriage. And there is no more serious and painfully tender tribute to his lifelong love for his wife than the memoir he wrote of her in the days after her death—a memoir he said was meant alone for his children and grandchildren (see Chapter 7). That his letters to her throughout their marriage were emotionless and bland may be attributed rather more to their perfect understanding of each other than to a lack of feeling, is Charles Brown's view: "It is as if the two were so well attuned that it was unnecessary for him to express his love for her." In Fanny's letters to Bryant and in her diary, there is evident a warmth of feeling, reticent though it is, that makes their understanding love even more apparent.

The Bryants set up housekeeping in Great Barrington, and the new husband kept up the practice of law. He acquired another interest at this time, beginning the study of political economy. The study instilled the principles he was to espouse during a half century in journalism.

In 1823, he took an offered opportunity to make regular contributions to the U.S. Literary Gazette, and in subsequent months, his poetic output was one of the most prolific of his life. In this period he also wrote for the North American Review, and began a long career of critical writing that was initiated in 1819 by an essay that was a critique of Solyman Brown's appraisal of American writers. The critique was acute in content and in itself considered to be a better evaluation of American literature than Solyman Brown's. Bryant was in fact so astute in his critical writing that he alone of critics who read a poem supposedly written by Byron refused to believe the famed poet had written it. It was later proven that Byron had not. The essay on Brown proved to be a turning point in the development of Bryant's reputation as an evaluative and critical writer.

From the dusty
path there opens,
Eastward, an unknown way;
Above its windings, pleasantly,
The woodland branches play.

THE MUSE, THE LAW, AND POLITICS

BRYANT was finding his profession even less rewarding than usual. At the urging of friends, he made a trip to New York in 1823, to see about finding a literary berth that would enable him to abandon law and make a satisfactory living. The trip laid the groundwork for the move more than a year later, when he found the sort of job he sought, as editor of a literary magazine. Then, as now, though, success with a literary magazine was a matter of chance, and despite Bryant's best efforts, the magazine failed within a couple of years.

Nonetheless it was an exciting time for the Bryants, who had come from the small village of Great Barrington to live a far more cosmopolitan life in the city. Bryant's friendships with the Sedgwicks—Charles, Theodore, Henry and Catherine; and Richard Henry Dana—had not only brought the couple to New York, but brought them into contact with leading writers and artists of the day. They included writers James Fenimore Cooper, Washington Irving and Ralph Waldo Emerson, and artists Thomas Cole and Asher Durand. Some of those acquaintanceships developed into lifelong friendships for Bryant. The contacts he made then led him into a new field, at which he was consummately successful: lecturing. He was also being courted at this time by one of the owners of the Boston-published U.S. Literary Gazette to which he had previously been a contributor. One of the shareowners wanted Bryant to purchase a one-fourth interest in the Gazette and become its New York editor, with the stipulation that he would merge his failing publication with it. Bryant agreed, no doubt with misgivings and a low-key lament for his lost magazine.

At about the same time, he was offered the chance to become a temporary assistant editor of the New York Evening Post, a newspaper founded in 1801 by Federalist Alexander Hamilton. Bryant took it. It was perhaps fortunate that he did, for complications developed in the plans for the literary magazine, and Bryant, distressed that some of the magazine's owners wanted to renege on their intent to make the magazine a dual-based publication, with offices in New York and Boston, bowed out of the enterprise.

His temporary job at the New York Evening Post, had begun when its editor, William Coleman, was injured when a runaway horse threw him from his carriage. Bryant accepted the employment as an assistant on an interim basis. It became a career that would last through 50 years and would set the standards for radical advocacy journalism in the century to come. Like the law, journalism was not his ideal of a profession; in fact he described his decision in a letter to Richard Henry Dana by saying that he preferred "politics and a bellyful to poetry and starvation." It was the kind of statement that later critics have used against Bryant to denigrate his works; they seem to feel that pragmatism and poetry made poor companions. But at this time, Bryant was already acclaimed by his countrymen, both for his poetry and his ethical standards in his various occupations. If he had any doubts about his own poetic powers, these doubts were not reflected elsewhere. And, too, his decision for "politics and a bellyful" may have had roots in the need of a writer to have a forum for his views.

Whatever the reason was, over the half-century that followed, he gave his job the same devotion and passionate energy that he used to attack every chore, profession and interest. In the process he gained the respect, admiration and even the adulation of a public that had grown used to the cynical depredations of the robber barons and the politicians, and who found in Bryant their champion and an opponent of special interests.

During his editorship, Bryant came to advocate the doctrines of free soil, the right to strike and to form unions for worker protection, and to oppose slavery, the entrenched rich and the robber barons. In fact, Bryant wrote what probably is the classic rhetorical argument for collective bargaining. In an editorial in the New York Evening Post, he said:

"Can anything be imagined more abhorrent to every sentiment of generosity and justice than the law which arms the rich with the legal right to fix by assize the wages of the poor? If this is not slavery, we have forgotten its definition. Strike the right of associating for the sale of labor from the privileges of a freeman and you may as well bind him to a master, or ascribe him to the soil."

Flying in the face of strong national feeling, Bryant opposed the doctrine of Manifest Destiny, which he felt could not be tenable in conscience if it worsened human condition. He believed that Manifest Destiny precluded a belief in a personal, all powerful Providence enlisted in a struggle for justice if in truth the struggle consisted of one part of a nation in contest with another section of the nation over enslavement of men. Bryant was fervently opposed to slavery. He sent so many communications of his opinions to President Lincoln that after the nation's leader signed the Emancipation Proclamation he was reported to have directed aides: "Tell Bryant I have freed the slaves."

Through all the years of his editorship, the New York Evening Post prospered while Bryant chafed, always wondering whether he had bypassed his true vocation for a life in the marketplace. But his firm editorial stances and his radical policies and politics greatly influenced his era, changing and enhancing the lives of his countrymen. It could truly be said of him that his life, and his ideals—radical, and ahead of their time— had as much effect as if he had been an elected leader of the republic he supported and revered his life long.

Through the Presidencies of 14 men, and through varied careers, he served well and faithfully. His side interests ranged from botany and municipal reform to mythology and homeopathic medicine; he was as assiduous in their pursuits as in those which earned him a living. He carried on an extended and thoughtful correspondence with almost every President from Jackson to Hayes, as well as with members of their cabinets, and of the Congress, writing 500 letters alone to the literati of his day and more to his intimates. In his daily work at the New York Evening Post, he hired men more liberal in their beliefs than he was himself. William Leggett, custodian of the editor's chair when Bryant traveled, was more radical than the radical editor-in-chief. Bryant, loyal to a fault, always supported Leggett in his clashes.

For fifty years he instructed, cajoled, scolded, or upbraided in his editorials, during an era when New York had three other dailies guided by
editors James Gordon Bennett of the Tribune, Horace Greeley of the

Herald, and Henry J. Raymond of the Times. Bryant's standards were high, both in form and in content. He stood foursquare for freedoms he believed to be the right of every American: free speech, the right to assemble, freedom from bondage, free trade, and the right of workers to unionize. He insisted on precision and clarity in writing. He taught by example and precept, suggesting projected revisions in copy gently and with tact. He never ducked an issue, confronting it though it be costly, painful, or complex, but he did hold himself apart from meeting the prominent persons of the day about whom he might someday have to write.

Bryant's characteristic loyalty to his friends extended also to his business partnerships, and the later New York Evening Post years were a period of considerable anguish to him and to his family. The pain was due to a belief by some that his partner, Isaac Henderson, was finagling to wrest control of the paper from him. The contretemps was complicated by the fact that one of those who tried to convince Bryant was Parke Godwin, who worked for Bryant at the New York Evening Post for some years until he married Bryant's daughter Fanny in 1842. Though his biographers say little about Bryant's attitude toward Godwin, it is generally agreed that though he stood mute on the subject, he was not happy with the alliance. Godwin left the New York Evening Post shortly after he and Fanny were married, but came back to the staff years later when the Henderson issue came to a head.

Certainly Bryant's extant correspondence indicates a closer relationship with his younger daughter, Julia, than with Fanny, though the affinity for Julia seems to have predated Fanny's marriage to Godwin. A friend of the Bryants' said of Fanny, "Somehow she always seemed to remember that she was the daughter of the great poet. She was in no way like her mother. His references to Fanny in letters to his wife, or to others were cooler in tone than those to Julia. And it was Julia who never married, and who, after her mother's death, was her father's traveling companion and housekeeper.

Godwin, in his voluminous biography of Bryant, referred not at all to Henderson, though it had been discovered just before Bryant's death that Henderson had either mismanaged or wrongfully charged against Bryant the sum of $200,000. Henderson had been the financial manager of the Post for a number of years, and had bought one third of its stock in 1854. He had started with the New York Evening Post in 1839 for the salary of $7 a week.

When the issue came to a head in 1878, Henderson agreed to sever his connection with the New York Evening Post and control of the paper reverted to Bryant, who had throughout refused to listen to any criticisms of Henderson, despite what his family and friends felt was tangible evidence that he was being wronged by his partner. Throughout his stewardship at the New York Evening Post, Bryant continuously complained that journalism satisfied him not at all. However, there is an account, written by an unidentified reporter for the Harper's New Monthly Magazine of an interview he'd had with Bryant, which indicates that the editor was perhaps not so loath as he professed to be.

"You will permit me to express my surprise that one whose thoughts are ever amidst green fields and budding flowers, and who has so keen and joyous an appreciation of the beauties of nature, should be content to immure himself in the dusky apartments of an editor, or mingle in the contemptible wrangles of party strife," the reporter said.

Bryant didn't answer, and his correspondent turned to political topics. Then Bryant took up the reporter's original question, almost as though the reporter had not spoken.

"You asked me a short time since what could induce me to remain in the midst of party struggles when a more tempting field awaited me, and you have already given my reply. Think you that the final triumph of political principles which long years have been spent in endeavoring to establish, frequently under the most disheartening circumstances, is not a sufficient reward for all my editorial toil?"

That was an unusual admission for Bryant, who sighed and groaned when he was forced to return from a European voyage because Leggett had fallen ill. He wrote to his friend Dana then, "I am chained to the oar for another year at least. . . " But after he bought Cedarmere, his grumblings about life in the marketplace fell away to occasional murmurings; the prodigious energies that he used to such wide advantage, on so many levels, seemed to be more highly charged than ever. At the same time, it appeared to afford him the chance he needed to maintain a contemplative life in the midst of the tumult.

A silvery
brook comes stealing
from the shadows of its trees,
Where slender herbs of the
forest stoop
Before the entering breeze.

LONG ISLAND REDWOOD

SOMEWHERE at Cedarmere is a seed, or a memory of a tree, that grew first in the Mammoth Grove of California. Some seeds, along with a piece of the bark and cone, were sent to Bryant by a woman emigré from Europe who was visiting there. Her first thought, she wrote in an accompanying letter, was of his poem, "Forest Hymn." She said she remembered the first line: "The groves were God's first temples," as she gazed in awe at the giant trees. "Three thousand years of life!" she wrote to Bryant.

21

She explained that many of the trees in the grove were named for great men of American history—Webster, Clay, Grant, Sherman and Lincoln—but she was disappointed to find that there were no trees named for a poet. She wanted to honor Bryant. She inquired about the possibility and said she found that the procedure was simple: a marble tablet with the name inscribed could be sent to the grove, and the donor was to select the tree to be named.

"Accordingly," she said, "I selected the second tree at the right hand of the path very near the entrance of the grove, a very old tree, one of the largest, and one that has not only braved the storms of centuries, but which has felt the scourge of the savage-fire. It is a splendid specimen of a great old age, still strong, still fresh, the birds yet singing in its lofty top, a fitting emblem of the poet of the forest, Bryant."

Whether the California redwood which withstood three thousand years of history could father a tree to withstand Long Island weather is moot, but Bryant duly planted the seeds, as he did all such offerings. He was modest, however, in his letter of thanks, wondering if public opinion would have been so partial to his selection as the first poet to be so honored. Bryant was ever aware of his place in time, and deprecated his accomplishments. Besides, he said he did not wonder that political and military celebrities should be honored. "The events of the last four years (the Civil War) have kept the public attention fixed upon the actors in our political stage, and the gallant deeds of our commanders in the war have for the moment at least thrown all other kinds of fame into the shade."

Along
those pleasant windings
I would my journey lay,
Where the shade is cool and the dew of night
Is not yet dried away.

TALISMAN

TREES loomed always in Bryant's thoughts and memories, figuring as important in his life as in his writing, whether he was writing editorials to promote a park for New York City, or purchasing rare varieties for planting at his home, or writing a poem. The trees in his mind seemed as much a talisman of the continuity and renewal of the world as they were an objective reality on his grounds. He believed that man is just part of the endless atoms—trees grow from the decay of their predecessors.

23

The redwood may not have flourished to spread its massive contours over a plot of ground at Cedarmere, but myriad other species did, to the bemusement of visitors, then and latter-day. A visitor could be hard-taxed to put names to all the species; Bryant was not. He had become an accomplished horticulturist—building bountiful gardens of flowers and trees from seedlings and cuttings sent as gifts or bought from countries all over the world. On the grounds grew two kinds of persimmon trees, a Portuguese quince, a chickasaw plum, and a Chinese sand pear, four or more varieties of native pear, apples, cherries and mulberry, nuts of all kinds and ornamental and flowering trees and shrubs.

"The trees of Cedarmere present a curious combination of natural wildness with artificial planting. Not far from the house stands a Turkish oak, brought from Greece," wrote one reporter. "A visitor on one occasion commented to Mr. Bryant upon the shapeliness of a huge European elm standing near by. 'Would you believe me,' responded the poet with animation, 'if I should tell you that I brought that tree, a feeble sapling, from Oyster Bay, in a one-horse wagon, twenty-nine years ago?' Then, springing forward with boyish elasticity—he had already passed his eightieth birthday—he ran lightly up the bank and stood by the great trunk of the tree. 'See!' he exclaimed, 'how the sapling has outgrown man!' "

But trees were more than and less than talismens. The consummate horticulturist knew their natural value. In an essay called "The Utility of Trees," Bryant wrote:

"We are fully persuaded, for our part, that scarce anything is more prejudicial to the fertility of a country or has a worse effect on its climate, than the thoughtless practice of denuding it of trees. The effect is to open the region to the winds which parch the surface and dwarf the vegetation to cause the springs to dry up, and turn the water courses into torrents in the rainy season and dusty channels in summer and autumn. If the public could but be thoroughly convinced of this truth, it might perhaps be unnecessary for the government to give itself any concern about the matter in the disposition of the public lands. We should see the highways skirted by double rows of trees, long lines of plantation following the courses of the railroads, belts of forest-trees planted to break the force of the winds and shelter the tender crops and the orchards which bear fruit."

He was exacting in selecting the proper spot for shrubs, flowers and trees, pruning and moving them to help their growth. On occasion he transferred them from one of his homes to another, and replaced those which died or were sickly and unresponsive to his ministrations. And he exulted in their flourishings. In a letter to a friend he wrote, "In this chilly weather, I suppose you do not regret your return to the city. Yet the cool days and nights have given a long blooming time to the fruit trees and with your keen enjoyment of the beautiful in nature, you could endure the inclemency of weather for its sake."

24

Flowers too were his delight. In 1870, Bryant wrote a careful list of the garden flowers "in bloom at Roslyn, October 13, 1870. No frost yet." There were 38 listed, from the ubiquitous rose to sweet alyssum, China pink, althea, petunia, lantana, European violets, salvia, fuschia and Japanese anemones. Midway in the second column of the list was an unexpected entry: "unknown." Six days later, he added a note: "Oct. 19th. No frost yet at Roslyn. To this list now add the chrysanthemum."

He was usually less businesslike in his description of his gardens. "I find the season of flowers already begun," he wrote lyrically to one correspondent. "The forsythias are in gorgeous bloom, the ground is sprinkled with blue and white violets, and the daffodils are wagging their yellow heads at my door."

In a contemporary account of a "pilgrimage" to the poet's home in 1870, an author and friend of Bryant's, I. Marvel Mitchell, described Cedarmere as it appeared to the visitor:

"The weather is doubtful as the little steamer Sewanhaka nears the dock at Great Bay (possibly Great Neck). It is questioned if we should take the open carriage, which is drawn up and waiting, or run out by boat to the bay of Roslyn; but the voice of that one of the party who would seem least able to brave storms decides for the drive, and away we go through the pleasant roads that skirt the north shore, now brushing the boughs of a veteran wood, now rounding a placid inlet of the Sound, passing scant, quiet hamlets, old country homesteads, orchards, grain fields, wayside churches, seven miles or more, until we rattle down into the little village of Roslyn.

"Passing through the village and bearing north, we have at our right a bold, wooded bluff, and at our left a spit of land between the high road and the quiet bay, which there juts with a southward sweep into the Long Island shore. Upon this spit of land are scattered houses—three of which, by their orderly keeping, mark the beginning of Mr. Bryant's property. Farther on, the land between the road and the bay widens so as to give room for a couple of placid little lakelets, lying so high above tidewater as to supply a raceway for a picturesque mill which stands on the farther shore of the northern pool, embowered in trees. The lands sloping to this pool are lawn-like in keeping, and a swan or two with a brood of ducks are swimming lazily over it; a post bridge spans the narrowed part, and a skiff lies moored under a boathouse under the northern bank. Eight or 10 rods beyond, under the shadow of a great locust and a tulip tree, we catch a glimpse of the homestead. The carriage comes to a stand under a bower of shade.

"Along the walk we pass on and up the broad veranda, which sweeps along around three sides of the homestead. No martinet-like precision shows in the keeping of either lawn or walks; everywhere turf and garden carry the homelike invitingness of look which testifies to the mastership of one who loves the country and its delights.

"Within doors a great welcoming blaze is upon the parlor hearth: a provision against the damp evenings of early June: piquant souvenirs of 25 wide travel arrest the eye, dashes of watercolor, which friendly artists have contributed to the cheer of the master; a bit of ruin which may be the Roman forum, a blaze of sunset which may hover over the blue waters of Capri, or haply a stretch of the Rhône at Avignon, over the mantel a photograph from the fresco of the wonderful 'aurora' of Guido. In the library, no affectations of literary aplomb, or of literary disorder, but only markings of easy, everyday comfortable usage, maybe a little overheaping of such reference books as go—just at this date—to the furnishing or mending of the translation of Homer."

Path of the
flowery woodland!
Oh whither
dost thou
lead,

HYACINTHS FOR THE SOUL

RYANT was generally poetic in his writings about Cedar mere. Urging his lifelong friend Mrs. Leonice Moulton (from whose husband he had bought the estate) to take up tenancy there, he extolled the virtues of visiting over ownership, apparently so she would feel free to come and stay. "Yours are the fresh air and the sunshine and the grateful shade of trees and the verdure of the fields and the (unclear: perhaps hues) and fragrance of the flowers, and the sparkle and murmur of the waters, just as much as if you had 40 acres to worry over. Your husband goes down on Saturday to see his old place and I daresay will take more pleasure in it than when he owned it."

Moulton had made changes in the plain old Quaker house, and Bryant had made more. He added bay windows, and new verandas with doors opening off both the first and second floors. Then he decorated the balconies on both floors with climbing vines, honeysuckle, clematis and cadea. Inside, wrote Theodore Wolfe in "Literary Haunts and Homes of American Authors," was "a spacious hall with an ancient stair; Dutch doors at either end extend through the centre of the house. On its right is the dining room, opposite the parlor, with an ample fireplace and an antique stone hearth on the side wall." The library, Wolfe said, was just back of the parlor—the place to which Bryant retired when "he donned his singing robes." The library had twin bay windows, one with a view of the flower-decked slopes that led to the harbor, and the other with a magnolia tree in view.

Bryant never stopped tending, dressing and reordering his lands, and his house. He continued to purchase property surrounding his until he owned over 200 acres. His love for having visitors urged him into adding guest houses to the estate, from the house between the artificial lake and the harbor that he had built for Fanny and Godwin, to the other cottages on the estate, until there were numerous outdwellings, most of which remain standing. Some were sold and are in use as private residences today.

His friends and family had open invitations to Cedarmere, where the doors to the main house were open in constant hospitality. So were the cottages when they were unrented, so that Bryant could have about him companions to share his delight in his home.

"Come and sun yourselves awhile like venerable snakes here at Roslyn before you turn yourselves into your den for the winter," Bryant wrote to his friend Dr. Orville Dewey, who had, with his sister, Jerusha, a virtual lease on one of the cottages. "The line gales have blown themselves out of breath and the sun is hurrying off as fast as he can go toward the winter solstice, but in the meantime he is pouring out a flood of golden sunshine that we prize all the more because, on account of the shortening days, we get less and less of it every 24 hours. The warm sunshine is never so sweet as when a frosty air stands in close neighborhood to it."

Wandering
by grassy
orchard-grounds,
Or by the open
mead?

CEDARMERE—A PLACE IN TIME

VISITOR who alighted from ferry or stage coach to spend a week, a month or a year at Cedarmere, as time permitted, had a horticultural panorama to delight in and a various parcel of amusements to choose. These ranged from Bryant's beloved rambles to springtime strawberry festivals, which were frequent events also for the neighborhood children. The youngsters were invited for special occasions of their own, a testament to Bryant's delight in and love for children. There was a summertime equivalent of the spring festivals, too, when the grapes and gooseberries ripened. It was the time for gay summer forays into the woods and fields to gather roots for homemade root beer. 29

And there were walnuts to gather, persimmons and cherries and plums to pick. Even now, on the grounds of Cedarmere, rhubarb beds and formal gardens, and, a greenhouse, untended, still are testimony to Bryant's skill.

Bryant's friend Charles Sedgwick, in an amusing 1855 thank-you note, sent after a visit by himself and his sister Catherine, said his visit had been refreshing. "I came back in heart and head so much better than I went that I could hardly help thinking that the Lord blessed everything and everybody at Roslyn with one exception: He taketh no delight in the *legs* of a man, the very thing, and almost the only thing, one wants there, for brain and everything else is supplied on the spot. My children inquired of me about the house and place, and the youngest, of course, about the furniture, and all I could describe was something of the garden and the trees—grand and beautiful . . ."

Sedgwick was not the only visitor who lamented the shortcomings of his stamina, for Bryant's legs seemed not to feel the fatigues that affected those of his guests, including those of persons much younger than he. Walkers with Bryant were put to severe tests, for he was said to be as agile and strong in the eighth decade of his life as he had been as a young man. One of his visitors, Horatio Nelson Powers, visited Bryant in Cummington after the poet had bought back the old family home in 1865. He recalled a stroll in which Bryant, at the age of 82, indulged himself and sorely taxed Powers, who had come to interview Bryant for a magazine article. "I had walked with him a long way," Powers wrote, "and after crossing a wide desolate field full of briers, we came to the sunny side of an old wood, whose border for some distance was a thick tangle of wild rank weeds, as high as our heads. The day was hot, and the struggle to break our way through this mass of vegetation very fatiguing, after all our previous exercise. Having succeeded, we reached, a little way within the forest, a large log, which looked pleasantly inviting as a seat, and the luxury of which I really wished to enjoy. Said I, 'Mr. Bryant, here is a good place for us to rest; shall we sit down for a while?'

" 'If you are tired,' he replied, 'we will do so; if not, let us go on.'

" 'I need hardly say that our walk was continued,' Powers said, "and he seemed fresh at its very end.' "

The incident points up Bryant's power for compelling others by example. He spurred companions on to greater physical exertions just as he encouraged his assistant editors at The New York Evening Post to harder, higher efforts by his own drive.

He spoke of drive and energy as an effect of climate in an article in The New York Evening Post on March 1, 1932, writing,

"As respects the moral effects of our climate, there is nothing to complain of. The inhabitants of lands blessed with a soft and equable temperature are apt to be voluptuous. The people of less genial regions have made the greatest advances in civilization and carried the arts and sciences to their highest perfection. Labor is never loved for its own sake; men require severe necessity or some desire to sting them into activity.

"Our climate, while it presents many of the beautiful phenomena of those which are reckoned the finest, is yet (for the truth must be acknowledged) variable, capricious and severe, and extracts more ingenuity and foresight in guarding against the extremes to which it is subject than almost any other."

Invariably, Bryant's biographers noted his love of the walks that offered him solace, the chance to delight in the woods and plains and streams, with the enhancement of keeping trim and vigorous. One friend recalled Bryant's preference for walks through wild countryside. "He was the most indefatigable tramp I've ever grappled with. A baker's biscuit and a few apples seemed to suffice him for food, and he put up cheerfully with the rude fare of wayside inns and laborers' cottages. His knowledge of soils and seasons, his interest in agriculture and the modes of life and opinions of farmers soon got him into pleasant chats with the people he encountered," another friend wrote. Other contemporaries of Bryant recalled his unending curiosity and love for chatting—in his travels and on his walks at home, he rarely missed an opportunity for gossip with farmers, stage-drivers and woodsmen.

On his journeys, too, he was constantly awake to opportunities to get to know the countryside and its people, avoiding the city hotels with their international ambience, and opting for the country instead. He stayed at small inns where he could mingle with the local inhabitants, and learn about the country's customs. His travel journals were clear, detailed accounts of what he saw, and are valuable records of the foods, greenery, customs and habits of the places he visited.

Bryant's tenderness for every living thing was an extension of his keen powers of observation, that very perceptiveness which enabled him to observe a single blade of grass or one yellow violet among the myriad made him take joy in the singularity of each living thing and helped him towards that great sensitivity that his friends so valued in his nature. Robert Waterston, in a tribute written after Bryant's death, remembered a stay at Roslyn in which he and Bryant were examining some trees near the house. Waterston saw that a large branch on one tree had been sawn nearly through, so that its own weight would have forced it to fall. But the event had been forestalled by the simple expedient of having the limb shored up with bracing ropes which were woven through the other branches to fasten it to the trunk and higher branches.

With a smile, Bryant explained. "My gardener came to the conclusion that the absence of this bough would be an improvement to that tree. The work of destruction was at once commenced when his purpose attracted 31 my notice. On that branch,' Mr. Bryant said, pointing beneath the leaves, 'you will see a nest, where the parent birds had been watching their young. I instantly ordered the gardener to bring ropes and have the branch carefully secured in its place. It was an awkward thing to accomplish, but he has at least succeeded sufficiently well to leave the birds undisturbed, which is a great satisfaction, and this accounts for what you see."

Bryant's long affection for the woods had its roots in his childhood affinity for solitary walks, and even before he reached young manhood the feeling had evolved into a sense that man was in harmony with nature. It affected his outlook so strongly that he could go to great lengths to foster and to protect that harmony. Another of Powers's reminiscences of Bryant was of an incident in which the poet expressed his distress at a guest's insensitivity. Visitors always were invited to share in the fruits of his labors at Cedarmere, but there were limits. At no time were Bryant's friends encouraged to fish. Powers said a guest had cut down a stick from the shrubbery on the lawn, and put it to use as a makeshift fishing rod, to angle in the little lake. When Bryant saw what he was doing, he stopped him instantly, and not alone because the rod the fisherman had chosen was "a rare and precious young sapling," but because Bryant could not bear the thought of anyone inflicting pain on the fish.

Powers also said that Bryant's gentleness had made him abandon an expressed plan to erect a swing on the schoolhouse grounds at Cummington, after Powers told him that swings were dangerous and could cause serious accidents. But Bryant's joyous nature must have triumphed at Cedarmere, for Wolfe mentions a swing on the grounds there. Powers's note that Bryant acquiesced in the prohibition of a swing seems an overly cautious act on the part of a man who swung over tree branches and did strenuous calisthenics even in his eighties.

There were many such conflicts in the various views of Bryant among his friends and biographers; he was seen as aloof and arrogant, or guarded and diffident. A more comprehensive view was drawn by a writer for Munsey's Magazine, who believed that Bryant, often acrimonious in his editorial writings, avoided contact with the political persons of his day. He did this, the writer declared, to avoid bringing along with him in personal affairs the prejudices that would have caused intemperate behavior in individual encounters. But in his relationships with trusted intimates, the writer said, Bryant "lavished his best and truest social nature."

One of Bryant's neighbors at Roslyn recalled this social, loving nature. Eliza Seaman Leggett, in a journal written in her old age at the request of one of her grandchildren, Eleanor Randall, spoke of Bryant as a man who was affectionate and loving to children, and considerate and caring in his relations with friends and family. Her journal was found in a Boston bookshop many years by Mrs. Barbara Sprague of Michigan after it was

written. She gave it to another famous Roslyn author, Christopher Morley, who turned it over to the Bryant Library. In it Mrs. Leggett told anecdotes that bring new insights about the Bryants of Cedarmere.

The Leggetts' daughter Anna was newborn and not yet named when Mrs. Bryant had called on Mrs. Leggett and asked her to join them on a walk in the woods. The Bryants were invited into the cottage, where Bryant picked up the baby and asked what the Leggetts meant to name her. ". . . Call her Anneta. It is such a sweet pretty name, and it means Anna just the same," Bryant said. Mrs. Leggett said he always called the baby Anneta after that.

Mrs. Leggett's husband offered to care for the infant so that she might go along for the walk. She wrote:

"It was a long uphill walk, perhaps a half mile from our front door, to the beautiful spot we wanted to reach at the top of the hill. Then we came to a large field of grain, but it had a nice space for walking at the side, all bordered with trees and sheltered by vines of the bittersweet, full of the pretty berries—yellow blossoms and the highest centres. Then we walked under the trees and these pretty clinging vines and came to a lovely spot where we could look down upon the village and see the busy and bustle of the little place—loud laughter and happy sounds. Mr. Bryant read to us from the Berkshire (manuscript unclear: evidently a book or paper). His shoes had some breaks in them and altogether he had planned for the woods. Then came Mrs. Bryant's nice 'biscuit' and it was time to come home. As we came back, Mr. Bryant said, 'We must take home some trophies from our walk—some of this lovely bitter sweet. Then he tore the vine down—oh! immense lengths."

They wound it around him, from his head to below his knees, letting loose ends dangle, like tassels. "And," Mrs. Leggett wrote, "he danced around like a boy all the way down the hill until we got near 'civilization.' " They unwound the bittersweet and made a wreath of it for Bryant to carry home on his arm. Mrs. Leggett said that Fanny Bryant told her, " 'Always William is a boy in the woods.' Once she told me she never saw him happier than when he went with us."

But he appeared able to maintain that boyish attitude even when he wasn't in the woods. Mrs. Leggett, the daughter of Dr. Valentine Seaman and possibly a descendant of Richard Kirk, the builder of Cedarmere's mansion, also recalled a time when she and her husband called on the Bryants on a Christmas evening. "Mrs. Bryant showed me the handsomest book of the Mother Goose that I have ever seen," Mrs. Leggett wrote.

" 'William bought me this for my Holy Day Gift,' " Mrs. Bryant said. Mrs. Leggett noted that the inscription in it read, "I have never yet met a book that has given me so much delight, and I present it to you to recall the happy days of childhood."

Bryant himself told Mrs. Leggett he believed the education of a child is unfinished unless he or she knows every verse of Mother Goose and when he first heard the verses in childhood, he "believed every word of it was true."

Mrs. Leggett also contributed a different amplified version of the traditional story of the way in which the little village of Roslyn was named. It was once called Hempstead, and there were numerous areas of the island with the same name, like Hempstead Harbor, and Hempstead Branch. "One can easily see how bewildering this was to a stranger," Mrs. Leggett wrote.

Entertainment in those times was made of simple pleasures, and residents of the hamlets and towns of rural America often invited lecturers to come and talk to them. "We entertained all the lecturers we could, for they were generally pleasant, well-informed persons, and we had very little society outside of the village . . . one time came a Scotchman, and we invited him to stay with us. (He was a) most interesting person, so we had a great delight for a few days, and your grandpa told all the old stories he knew and listened quite pleased to the Scotchman. One day he (the visitor) said, "You have too many towns called Hempstead. It is bewildering. If you ever want to change the name call it Roslyn—it is very like old Rosslyn in Scotland. Well, in the course of time, a meeting was called and held in our house, no ladies invited." She told her husband to save his vote to the last, and sat in the room close to him "with my foot to his sensitive toe." It was a small gathering.

"I was so intent on the name Roslyn. Mr. Bryant thought it would be good to call it Hill Town."

The men deliberated and smoked their pipes. "I sewed diligently and innocently. One more vote would make it Hill Town, and one more would make it Roslyn."

For all Mrs. Leggett's admiration of the poet, she could not admire his mundane choice of a name, and she would not give in. When her husband whispered to her, "Bryant thinks Hill Town, why not?' " Mrs. Leggett's response was to give him "such a twinge on the gouty toe." The name came to be Roslyn, but it seems reasonable to assume the poet's status in the village which might have influenced the choice was overcome by a well-placed kick to a gouty toe, which caused Mr. Leggett to exclaim in pain. His cry was interpreted as a vote for Roslyn.

Mrs. Leggett's entry for that incident concludes "And now the pretty harbor town delights to have been named for the poet Bryant's vote, and are so glad to think this is the truth, and I am willing, but it was the Scotchman who gave me the name, and my foot that hurt Grandpa's toe, that its pretty name came." That is a version with a likely ring to it, and has a wholeness that the generally quoted story—that the British marched out of Roslyn and of Long Island to the tune of Rosslyn Castle—does not have.

Mrs. Leggett also delineated Bryant's homely and unassuming nature in another anecdote she recounted for her granddaughter. "Mr. and Mrs. Bryant liked to walk over to see us, and we always urged them to stay to tea, but it did not need much urging." On one visit the table was set. "Old Dorcas, when she found the company had come, took off the apple pie, but Augustus (your Grandpa) had seen it, and pretty soon said, 'Why, where's the apple pie?'

" 'Oh,' said Dorcas, who was peeping at the door to hear what they would say about her nice tea, 'Why, when the quality came I thought it sort of not so nice to have the pie and so got out our best preserves.'

" 'Oh! let's have the apple pie,' said Bryant, and old Dorcas, with her long tow apron from her throat to her heels, sort of sniffed up her nose and bustled about, and somehow felt it was a mistake to put on one of her apple pies for quality, and was 'clear lifted off of her feet' when Bryant asked to take one home. 'La, for goodness sake, for the quality to like my apple pie,' she said.' "

Mrs. Leggett apologized to her granddaughter for writing as much as she did of the Bryants, but said she was "so often requested to do it," and that she liked to remember those days. Having known the couple from her childhood, she was familiar with the poet's more relaxed moods, and remembered him as a gentle and affectionate man: "the tiny little turtles he would bring me, and now and then blackberries in a leaf, oh, the biggest and the sweetest that ever were."

Mrs. Leggett's journal also affords glimpses of the relationship—affectionate and teasing—between the Bryants. Once, when Bryant had a visitor she called Professor Morse (the inventor of the telegraph, Samuel F. B. Morse, who had once painted a portrait of Bryant) Mrs. Leggett said Mrs. Bryant came to the door and putting her finger to her mouth to ask for silence, told Mrs. Leggett, 'Walk on tiptoe and see the two boys.'

"There, to be sure, at the back door, were the two 'boys,' " Mrs. Leggett recalled, ". . . sitting on a bent limb like all possessed."

Small, homely details such as these help offset Bryant's reputation as a cold and unapproachable man.

Goest
thou by
nestling
cottage?

NATURE OF THE MAN

EVERY day of his adult life Bryant practiced calisthenics, and lifted light barbells for a period of each morning. He never rode where he could walk, no matter how inclement the weather, and he would not tolerate weakness in his own flesh though he was especially tender in caring for others. He never complained of the hours he spent in tending Fanny during her last illness, and he was unfailingly kind in his dealings with persons who were ill. But he had no patience at all with infirmities of his own body. He once said he hoped for a day when health, like disease, would be catching.

When he was 80 years old he suffered a fall while he was walking to his office one rainy, icy winter day. In a letter to Miss C. Gibson, with whom he corresponded regularly, he said of that day, "It always seems to me that there is a kind of disgrace in falling to the ground. Drunken people fall. As I got up, I thought to myself, 'Nobody at least is here who knows me. At that very moment, a gentleman whom I did not know asked, "Are you hurt, Mr. Bryant?' 'Of course not,' I answered, and I marched off down town as if I had just come from my door."

Nor did he accept the disability which was the result of the fall. His shoulder was lame afterward, reminding him "now and then and not very importunately by neuralgic twinges and shootings of pain of the unlucky bruise which it had from my fall on Broadway."

In an account he wrote of his "Habits of Life" Bryant attributed his good health and vitality to temperate attitudes and vigorous exercise.

"I have reached a pretty advanced period of life without the usual infirmities of old age and with my strength, activity and bodily faculties generally in pretty good preservation," he wrote. ". . . I rise early at this time of the year (March) about half past five; in summer, half an hour or even an hour earlier. Immediately, with very little encumbrance of clothing, I begin a series of exercises designed to expand the chest . . . My breakfast is a simple one: hominy and milk or brown bread and grits, and in the season, baked apples, for animal food I never take at breakfast. Tea and coffee I never touch at any time. After breakfast I occupy myself with my studies, and then walk down to the Evening Post, nearly three miles distant, and after about three hours, return, always walking, whatever the weather . . . In the country I dine early and it is only at that meal that I take either meat or fish and of these but a moderate quantity, making my meals mostly of vegetables . . . sometimes, though rarely, I take a glass of wine. I never meddle with tobacco except to quarrel with its use. That I may rise early I of course go to bed early, in town at 10, in the country somewhat earlier . . . it was said that I was in the habit of taking quinine as a stimulant, that I depended upon the excitement which it caused in writing my verses . . . (but) I abominate all drugs and narcotics."

But Bryant did not ask his guests to abide by his own ascetic rules. A visitor at Cedarmere, who wrote that "one sees the man to greatest advantage" there, described both Bryant's physical appearance at 70 years old and his gracious manner as a host in an article in Harper's New Monthly Magazine, that was published during Bryant's lifetime. "To those who have had the opportunity of meeting him under his own roof he appears one of the pleasantest of companions. In person he is slight and from long habit in leaning over the desk and perhaps in part from an originally delicate constitution, is inclined to stoop, like one laboring from debility. His habits are regular, and he carries abstemiousness almost to a fault. While his breakfast table is amply supplied with suitable provisions for his guests, he contents himself with a frugal dish of boiled southern hominy and milk. He uses neither tea nor coffee, although he tacitly recommends them by presenting them to his guests."

Bryant told the visitor of his habit of taking exercise with dumb-bells, 37 and the correspondent was astonished. "Do you not think the exercise too violent for one of your temperament?"

"On the contrary," Bryant answered. "I derive the greatest benefits from their use. Whenever I intermit this exercise—which I seldom do—I feel stupid and heavy, but when my lungs are freely expanded by an hour's exercise, my frame seems nerved for any task I may be called upon to perform."

The discussion led into a conversation about weight, and Bryant had the last word: "I would infinitely prefer to carry a carpet bag for half an hour and then be relieved of the burden than to be obliged to support its weight with every step I took."

Good temper was as important to the man as was good health, but he was not, according to one account, "given to easy and uncalled for smiles and invariably weighed his words except in rare moments of vexation." He apparently made strong efforts to avoid vexation; he was wretchedly ashamed on the few occasions on which he lost his temper, including the times in court, as a young lawyer, when his self control vanished on provocation by his adversaries. Drunkards in particular elicited no sympathetic pangs in Bryant's nature; he was clearly intolerant of the vice even though he had no quarrel with spirits and did sometimes enjoy wine or beer. On one moonlit summer night in Roslyn Bryant quarreled and exchanged heated epithets with a man who was drunk. Later, according to a memoir, *Bryant the Traveler,* written by his friend J. Durand, Bryant was said to have berated himself harshly for not being more forbearing of his "fellow creature."

That great sense of rectitude and duty that demanded forbearance and caused him to rebuke himself, led him also to take extraordinary measures to repay even so small a debt as a dollar. It caused him to refuse honors and titles which he felt would be so demanding that he would not be able to do his best work, or to say yes to participation in affairs that he deemed unworthy. Bryant also judged himself harshly, because, as he wrote to Dana in 1824, he "recognized . . indolence and a spirit of procrastination which is my besetting infirmity."

Late in his life he had been chosen without his knowledge, as a New York State Regent for education by the New York Legislature. He declined, for, as he said in a letter to John Bigelow from Paris in 1858, he would find it difficult to combine the duties of the office with his other pursuits, and he had, moreover, an aversion to participation in any form of public life.

Bryant felt a deep sense of responsibility in all phases of his life, but most especially to his family. In a letter to his cousin Phebe in 1864 he thanked her for reminding him of his obligation to be charitable. She had written of another cousin, Abigail, who had become insane. Phebe's letter, he said, made him aware of his duty and he would now try to perform it by helping out financially.

He not only counseled his brothers on purchases of land in Illinois, both for themselves and for him, as investments, but he advised them also on personal matters. In a letter to one of his brothers, Bryant advised him to think carefully before choosing a wife, and to find someone who would share his interests. His letters to his daughters when they were children and traveling abroad with their mother were models of instruction. He urged them to be devoted in their studies, to absorb the languages of the countries they visited, and to bear out the importance of knowing more than one language, he would often write passages in French or Italian or Spanish as an encouragement to them toward translation. Not least of his admonitions to them was that they obey their mother in all things.

He was no less concerned for the welfare of his wife, always keeping a weather eye on the state of her financial records and making deposits to her accounts, often with instructions to her to deny herself nothing on her travels, even if such expenditures would strain the family wallet.

Another time, he was urged by many, including Whittier and Holmes, to write a biography of Abraham Lincoln. He refused, wisely noting that so great a task—the four years of Lincoln's Presidency and the turmoil of the Civil War—comprised more history than most wise men would want to tackle.

In a reminiscence of Bryant, his long time friend and fellow poet Richard H. Stoddard wrote of one of those acts of charity, which Bryant never mentioned but of which his friends were well aware. Stoddard said that one of the last times that he saw Bryant in the last days of the poet's life Stoddard had asked Bryant to read and criticize a poem he had written for a special occasion. Two or three days after Stoddard had given Bryant the poem, the two met again, and Bryant handed Stoddard a letter containing his criticisms. "I wanted to talk with him and would have done so but for the presence of one of our impecunious poets, who had evidently called upon him in the editorial room, and who had accompanied him into the business office of The New York Evening Post.

"I knew that a money transaction was about to take place, and not wishing for the honor of the guild to witness it, I left Mr. Bryant and his brother poet to themselves, noting as I did so that the hand of Mr. Bryant was in the act of slipping into his pocket. I folded up his letter, which was the last that he wrote, went away, and never saw him more, for in a week or ten days he was dead."

His personal philanthropies were more than matched by his public views and actions. In his *American Agitators, or Pen Portraits of Living American Reformers,* David W. Bartlett wrote in 1855, "Not merely as a poet or politician or an editor is Mr. Bryant distinguished. He is widely known as a philanthropist. His sympathies are always with the unfortunate and though from his retiring disposition he has had little to do with philanthropic organizations yet he deserves the esteem of all lovers of humanity   39 for his constant unwavering devotion to the welfare of his race." Another contemporary called him "intrepid, persistent, full of the love of justice and rich in human sympathies."

Bryant felt that the preservation of the union was essential to the preservation of the nation. In one of the letters to Lincoln in which he urged a more vigorous prosecution of the war, and criticized "the inactivity of our armies in putting down the rebellion," Bryant asked whether the country's citizens should then "resign ourselves to the melancholy conviction that the ruin of our republic is written down in the decrees of God?" And when Lincoln wrote him, in his own hand, to ask why Bryant had criticized him in the Post, Bryant replied, "You speak of having been assailed in the Evening Post. I regret that anything said of your public (manuscript unclear) should seem like an assault. The Evening Post always directs respectful criticism towards every successive administration . . . was not intending to proceed beyond those limits . . ." Not for a moment would Bryant bend the principles of his editorship, or his own code of ethical values.

He expected the same of others, and praised ethical behavior in others. To Mrs. Leonice Moulton he wrote in 1876, "As for yourself, I suppose you are doing good as usual, even if the occupation be so humble as feeding the chickens. To do good in the way that beneficence is wanted is the right thing, however apparently small the service may seem."

The clearest evidence of Bryant's loving nature and characteristic sympathy is seen in a spare and tender reminiscence of his wife as she lay on her deathbed. It speaks of what she meant to him, and is an unwitting tribute to him as much as to Fanny, of whom he said that she was "in all respects an example of goodness such as is rarely seen."

Bryant was away on a trip to Massachusetts when his wife, who had been ill for more than a year with a complaint that was probably heart disease, grew worse. He had been at Cummington, at the family's old homestead, which he had purchased in the hope that Fanny, if she could spend a summer in the highlands there might regain her strength . . . "I pleased myself with imagining how delighted my wife would be with the beauty of the situation, the charming prospect from the windows of the house, the neat and airy rooms, the pretty piazza and the well-centred arrangements . . ." Then he traveled to Pittsfield, Mass., to buy furniture "with a special view to her pleasure and as near as I could judge in conformity with her taste."

But a telegraph message reached him at Dalton in Massachusetts. "Mrs. Bryant is worse. Hasten home." He hurried—aboard two trains and then the Long Island Railroad, reaching Roslyn in a little over a day.

For the next 10 weeks, Mrs. Bryant lingered, suffering great pain, sleeplessness, nausea, breathing difficulties and a racking cough, Bryant said. Family members and friends nursed her day and night, one relative, a sister, staying by her bedside for 10 weeks.

Mrs. Leggett recalled that she was no longer living in Roslyn when Mrs. Bryant was sick. But Bryant came to her and said, "My wife is waiting impatiently to see you. She wants you to spend a few days with us." Mrs. Leggett had a house guest of her own, an uncle, Len Ives. He traveled with her to Roslyn, visiting a former neighbor while Mrs. Leggett spent a few days at the Bryant home, to cheer Fanny. Ives, she said, came early in the morning to Cedarmere to sit on the grounds and draw sketches of the place. "This pleased Bryant, and they enjoyed the few days we were in Roslyn together."

"In all this suffering she was exceedingly patient and unmurmuring. She uttered no groans, made no complaint against Providence, although the paroxysms of distress amounted to agony. She sometimes said to me, 'I know that you would do anything in the world to relieve me but you can do nothing. It is the will of God that I should suffer.' "

But Fanny could not always maintain her stoicism. "It were better that I should be released and go than to endure all this suffering," she cried once.

In the intervals between pain, Bryant read to her to "divert her mind from her constant bodily distress—prayers for the sick and other prayers, or repeated to her hymns." Fanny listened, and often told him of her interest, and the degree of intensity she felt toward the readings. "All that while her beautiful hands, which bore no marks of the disease that had wasted her sweet face, were spread out on the bed on each side of her, for she would not allow them to be covered by the bed clothes. Whenever I entered the room she extended one of them to me as if in sign of welcome. I could not refrain from kissing them whenever I came near them."

As Fanny lay dying, she begged Bryant, "You will come sometimes and see where they lay me?" Bryant pledged, "I need not record these dear words to remember while life lasts." Nor did he ever forget. He had built for her a memorial stone in the Roslyn Cemetery, where he is said to have purchased the first plot, and he visited her grave weekly, to strew flowers from his garden on the grave—"a green hillside," he later wrote, "enclosed by hedge of evergreen . . . in summer wind . . . soft airs, and song, and light, and bloom."

His memoir of Fanny includes a sketch of their life, and of their first meeting. "She was "a pretty blonde with hair of a rather light brown . . . grey eyes with a remarkable frank expression, an agreeable figure, a dainty foot, the prettiest hands, I thought, and the sweetest smile I had ever seen." Later acquaintance brought higher praise of her sweet disposition, her broad sympathies, her love for her family and her firm moral judgments. He cited her charities and said that one of the last acts of her life had been on such an errand. "I think it was the last time she drove out. . . The sexton of the little Presbyterian Church here, James Smith, had complained to me that he could hire no ground of his neighbors to cultivate a garden. My 41 wife immediately said, 'I will see to that.' The little wagon was brought up and we drove to the shop of William Valentine, owner of a piece of ground, then planted with potatoes, in front of Smith's house. "Will you let a little piece of your land to James Smith for a year if I pay the rent?" she asked. 'Certainly,' was the answer. 'Let us go then and look at it.' They went, Smith was called out, and asked how much land he would need. A small piece was staked off. 'What rent do you ask?' said my wife. 'I hardly know,' was the answer. 'Will ten dollars be high?' 'Quite,' was the reply. The money was paid and Smith has a flowering garden."

Fanny and Bryant were married for 45 years, and Bryant could say after her death that those many years as her husband led him to feel that the wedded life of few men had been happier.

"Few men have been so warmly beloved, and at the same time so wisely counselled. Strong as her affection for me was, it never made her blind to my failings, but rather prompted her to act the part of a kind and gentle monitor in aiding me to get rid of them. I have profited, I hope somewhat, both by her admonitions and her example. Who now will tell me with the same loving frankness, when I make myself disagreeable or ridiculous?

"She was my cheerful and unrepining helpmate in poverty and took its privations not as an evil but as an incentive to industry and the exercise of forecast. When in the decline of life we became more prosperous her chief pleasure in the change arose from the thought that her opportunities of doing good were enlarged by it. I think that she became more unselfish as she advanced in years, contrary to what is the common experience."

Fanny was no less tender, if modest, in her expressions of feeling for Bryant. In a letter she wrote to him while she was away on a visit, she said that she had read his last letter over and over again before going to bed, "it being Saturday night when I would so much like to be at home with you, and in truth I have staid here long enough. My visit is getting too long and I am impatient to be with you again." She went on to tell him of a tender little picture she had of him in her mind: through with his Sunday morning devotions and looking at the flowers in the garden. It was a reference to Bryant's habit of conducting worship services in the library at Cedarmere for his family, friends and employees on Sunday mornings.

Bryant's letters to Fanny and hers to him often included lyrical descriptions of weather and nature's offerings, almost as if the weather were a euphemism for their love for each other. Both loved the out-of-doors, and the house at Cedarmere was a physical expression of that love, with its wide verandas and many windows which almost brought the outside indoors. That sharing of a need for natural gifts gave the two modest lovers a natural topic in their letters. In 1855, Bryant wrote to Fanny of mundane things, stories about the villagers of Roslyn, news of his coming address before the New York Horticultural Society, and finally a note that indicated the gladness he felt at her planned return. The letter closes with a description of early autumn at Cedarmere.

In a reply full of concern for incidentals, occasional flashes of humor and human caring, she wished him well on the speech he was to make, described the weather as "cold and frosty," spoke of her brother, who was laying in supplies against the coming winter, and referred to a "frightful" accident on the railroad. Then, wistfully, because she wanted to come home, she asked him whether the grapes had ripened. But the next sentence was an abrupt dismissal of sentiment; she mentioned with a tinge of sarcasm that she "kept awake" at church services and heard a "pretty good sermon." There is no doubt she would have preferred to be present at Bryant's devotional service.

Fanny was much beloved by both her friends and Bryant's, and held in great esteem for her high standards and unchanging sense of justice. Julia was inconsolable when Fanny died, and Bryant, in a letter to his brother John, wrote of Julia's grief, and of how much she resembled her mother. Fanny was in Europe when her mother died. Both daughters, Bryant said, were very much attached to their mother—throughout her life they called her "Mamma By," for reasons Bryant did not explain. They were overcome at her loss.

Bryant's grief, poured out in the loving memoir he wrote in the days and weeks immediately following her death, never left him, though it took on other, less passionate forms. An ice house she had had built in 1845, while Bryant was in Europe was replaced by the poet in 1867 with a larger one. But as he explained in a letter to one of his brothers, he did not want to lose the first ice house, because it was Fanny's handiwork. He turned it into a cellar for storage. And he wrote often to friends and family of Fanny's goodness, and for himself wrote a short apostrophe to God thanking Him for Fanny's life and her gentleness. "And if it be the mission of departed souls to watch over those whom they loved while on earth, O, God, be pleased to assign me to her especial care for the short measure of life that remains to me and prepare me and mine to rejoin her in the land of the departed good. I ask it as an humble follower of thy love, Amen."

Though written in grief, it still can be seen as a positive answer to the poem he wrote called "Life.'"

"When we descend to dust again,
Where will the final dwelling be
Of thought and all its memories then,
My love for thee, and thine for me?"

So the tender pledges which Fanny and William made each other so many years before were fulfilled in their lifetime of shared devoted love, and left an abiding legacy of love for Bryant to draw upon after Fanny died.

Goest
  thou by
    stately hall
Where the broad
elm droops, a leafy dome
  and woodbines
flaunt on the wall?

FAIRY MUSIC

RYANT'S humor was at times dry, at times droll, particularly in later years, but he was also capable of broad strokes of humor. As a young man in Great Barrington, where he had few friends and despaired of finding compatible young company, he wrote to a friend, George Downes, in Bridgewater about his loneliness. He said that he felt melancholy because he was thinking of Worthington and "Ward's Store and Mill's tavern and Taylor's Grog Shop and Sears, J. Daniels's and Briggs and etc and etc and etc—such comfortable lounging places . . . for by the bye, there is not a tavern in this parish. A store with a hall, however, close to my door, supplies the place of one." Bryant was so poor at this period of his life that it is unlikely that he spent much time or money in grog shops, in Great Barrington or Bridgewater.

He tried to induce Downes to come to Great Barrington, telling him of a "fine great weekend" he had had with some friends. A planned ball had had to be put off for about a week because of continuing rain, but "at last despairing of ever having a clear sky we got together in a most tremendous thunderstorm and a very good scrape we had of it. I however was not manager of the next morning. We set out, six couples of us, to go to a great pond in Middleborough, about 12 miles from this place, on a sailing party which we had likewise been procrastinating a number of days on account of the weather. When we commenced our journey there was every sign of rain. The clouds were thick and dark and there was the devil of a mist. But the sun came out at about 10 o'clock and we had one of the most delightful days I ever saw. We had a charming sail on the lake and our ladies were wonderfully sociable and awake considering that they were up till 3 o'clock the night before . . ."

Bryant goes on to detail a previous letter he'd written to Downes which apparently hadn't been received. "In it, he said, "I mentioned that there was a whole army of them (beautiful Bridgewater girls) who were under my almost sole protection, and I promised you, Downes, if you would come and read law with Mr. Baylies I would make a liberal assignment of some half dozen to your share, more especially as I wanted to operate on only one at a time." This from a man who had lamented repeatedly the lack of social life in Bridgewater.

At the other end of his life, Bryant still was capable of drollery. He came home from a trip abroad with a caftan and the accoutrements to go with the Arabian costume, and of course, he had had a long beard for many years. He put the costume on to the startled astonishment of his neighbors in Roslyn. On one occasion he knocked at the door of a neighbor's house and when she came to the door he begged her for alms. She did not recognize him even when he engaged her in conversation, and was about to give him money when he, much amused, identified himself.

In a letter to Mrs. Moulton in 1849 he wrote, ". . . I was in hopes that by coming to town you would get into sober company and keep regular hours, but I perceive from some intimations in your letter that you are as wild as ever. Is it the force of habit or are you so agreeable that your friends there, as in the country, find their dissipations insipid without you and actually compel you to take part in them?"

Bryant's humor at times had a macabre cast. In another letter to Mrs. Moulton in 1862 he told her, ". . . Here we are in the midst of a general exultation at the defeat of the forces under Lollikoper in Kentucky, a newspaper editor formerly, then a member of Congress, next a rebel general, and now a corpse . . ." If that seems harsh, it is well to remember that Bryant was a staunch defender of the Union in the Civil War, and had chided 45

Lincoln for the "inactivity" of the Army. "We know little of the war (in Roslyn) save by rumor," he wrote to a friend, but he added that he and his family and friends prayed that "every part of the country would soon be as tranquil." The defeat of a rebel general would have hastened that time and would have seemed a cause for exultation. His letters to friends often were written in drolleries and some of the answers indicated that they were appreciated.

Once, in answer to a complaint from his friend R. H. Dana that Bryant was a bad correspondent, Bryant acknowledged the fault but wondered why Dana waited to hear before writing again. "I hold that in a correspondence it is the duty of each party to contribute according to his ability. Now as you are a practical and experienced author, fertile in intellectual resource with a host of fine ideas at your command, and a rich (this was crossed out and the word "ample" was substituted) wardrobe of fine dresses for them, if you were to write two letters to my one, you would hardly do your share."

Had he seen a letter that Bryant wrote in 1863 to the Reverend Dr. Orville Dewey, and remembered the 1822 letter, Dana might have asked Bryant for three for one. "Dear Doctor of Divinity," Bryant wrote to Dr. Dewey. "There are three D's for you—three semilunar fardels, as Dr. Cox called them, one more than you ordinarily get. You see what a fine thing it is to be of a munificent disposition, and to have ready a surplus of capital letters to bestow on one's friends upon proper occasions. I did not intend so soon to 'trouble you with a line," as a hangman once said to an unfortunate subject of his art." Perhaps only H. L. Mencken exceeded Bryant's ability to speak aptly and humorously, with so fortuitous a choice of words and phrases.

In another instance Bryant wrote about a legal case he had been involved with. He noted wryly that a client had: sworn not to leave the country; was unable to pay a debt at present but would pay if given time; and finally that the client intended before long to call and make some arrangement of the affair. "I believe," Bryant said, with some dryness, "that one item of information is true—namely, that he does not mean to pay the debt at present."

In one tongue-in-cheek poem that Bryant wrote as a valentine to Mrs. Moulton (it is interesting to note that many of Bryant's letters to her, especially during his middle years, had a decidedly romantic tone) he told her of how forlorn a place Roslyn was without her:

"Mrs. Moulton, I must say,
Since from Roslyn you departed
All its charms are fled away
All the dwellers broken hearted
And the sun that shone so bright
Sheds a sorry sort of light.
How, then, Madam, can a poet
Sing the beauty of the place?

It has lost and you must know it
All that gave it form and grace.—
All that made the springtime fair,
All that sweetened summer air.
Fairest of earth's sylphlike daughters,
With the high imperial brow,
Faintly glimmer now our waters,
Pallid are our roses now.
Your fresh cheeks and glances bright,
Gave the bloom—and gave the light."

Another time, in 1857, he answered a letter from Mrs. Moulton which had told him of a dream of hers. "I think," he wrote back, "you must have had a guilty consciousness of running away too soon from Roslyn, or you would not have been put to such hard service as you say you were in your dreams to improve the walks about my place."

He was ever urging her to return with warm descriptions of the weather, the flowers, and the creatures at Cedarmere, as in this fragment of an undated letter: "The country is now buried in snow, but in a day or two the birds and violets will be waiting for you at Roslyn."

Many of the letters to Mrs. Moulton, as to others of his correspondents, were descriptions of his horticultural efforts at Roslyn. He dispensed with preliminaries in one sentence by saying he had given her all the "gossip of Roslyn" that he had heard in a previous letter, and went on to talk about his trees. "The most remarkable thing, in my private opinion, which happened in the neighborhood this season, is that I had a young plum tree in the garden loaded with fruit which opened perfectly . . . I must have another of the sort. . . ." But it was evident he was aware of his single-mindedness about horticulture: he said in closing that they would discuss it when she returned because it was a "subject in regard to which you are most kindly patient with me."

Mrs. Moulton apparently once wrote to Bryant of a story she had heard of the reason for his success at horticulture: a story with a bit of a barb to it—that it was due to his wife's good advice and direction. He replied: "The report which you mention as affecting my good name does not disturb me. It is true enough that when I am at work in the garden I like to have Mrs. Bryant at my side, not on account of my ignorance of the proper method of putting seeds into the ground but for two other reasons. In the first place I do not like to work in the garden alone. In the second place I am partially indebted to you for the discovery of the fact that I must do as my wife says and how could that be if I had not her at hand to direct me?" The intonations of the letter, with its oblique reference to his indebtedness to Mrs. Moulton for learning that he must do as Fanny said, could be interpreted as a retrenching and reorganizing of the mood of the Bryant-Moulton relationship, or it could simply be taken as the surprising admission by Bryant that he needed someone, preferably Fanny, at his side while he accomplished the self-assigned task of landscaping and planting at Cedarmere. Whatever the reference and whatever the relationship between Bryant and Mrs. Moulton in the 1850s, his need for Fanny never flagged, and his awareness of his wife's goodness and loving nature never waned. He could write to his brother the day after her death, "Perhaps you did not know how strong and unerring was her sense of right and justice. It is not often, I think, that the two coexist in such perfection together."

It is no detraction from the many evidences of Bryant's constancy to Fanny, built on love and tender feelings as much as on the sternness of Bryant's moral attitudes born of his time and his upbringing, to note that he may have expressed his sense of the attractiveness of other women. It would have been more unusual if the poet had not expressed, poetically and intellectually, at least, so ardent a nature as his. Too, Mrs. Moulton had been his life-long friend. They shared a common background of childhood in the Berkshire hills of Massachusetts, where they had taken many long walks together, and she was a frequent guest of the Bryants after her husband sold them the Roslyn property. If the letters had an ardent compelling tone in the middle years of their correspondence, by 1876 they had softened into one of deep friendliness and appreciation of her friendship. Mrs. Bryant evidently shared those feelings, and often, Bryant said, urged him to write to Mrs. Moulton and press her to visit.

By steeps
where
children gather
flowers of
the yet fresh
year?

THE COMMUTER

STAGECOACHES were still a common mode of travel when Bryant responded to the 1842 advertisement that transformed him into a country squire. "... Situated in Hempstead Harbor," the ad said, "18-and-one-half miles from the city by way of Williamsburg and Flushing ... public conveyances to and from the city are by stage over the Flushing Turnpike, by railroad through Jamaica to Hempstead Branch (Mineola), thence by stage to and from the Harbour, and by steamboat to Glen Cove dock, within five miles of the place on the same side of the harbour. At present the boat runs no higher ..."

Bryant's friend Gulian Verplanck had urged him to buy on Long Island, 49 because it was within easy reach of Park Row. "The Brooklyn ferry has made the western tip of Long Island as convenient to New York as any place along the Jersey shore," he said. The Long Island Railroad was being built he said, and there would be plenty of island villages within easy access to the metropolis. Besides, he assured Bryant, the weather was cooler along the Sound than on the Hudson.

The stages were a necessary part of the components of travel to and from the city; during the nine months of the year when water travel was possible most travelers needed conveyance to the boat landings. And during the periods when the waterways were impassable in winter, the stages carried their commuting passengers to Mineola or other depots to meet the incoming trains.

It could not have been a very comfortable mode of travel, even though the stages themselves were imposingly handsome. In a contemporary account of travel on Long Island roads one author wrote that the roads were "exceedingly numerous and difficult for strangers." Three principal roads, called North, Middle and South, were intersected by roads leading from other towns and neighborhoods. Unfortunately, in uninhabited sections, the roads were little more than paths worn by the tracks of innumerable carts. Often the paths paralleled the main roads, and a traveler unfamiliar with the island could easily be led into strange byways, "where he might remain a whole day, without meeting a person to set him right." There were other "obstructions to locomotion," he wrote. "After a heavy rain, if only a single carriage has preceded you to open the ruts, you may get along with tolerable speed provided (which is a matter of great doubt) your wheels fit the track. But in a time of drought, the sand in many places is so fine, deep and fluid that you may travel for miles with the lower felloc of your wheels constantly buried out of sight."

Nonetheless, Bryant was prepared to put up with the ruts and bumps, and to take the stage when the ferry trip wasn't feasible. But railways were not his favorite way to travel. "I begin to think that railways, after all, are not the great things that some people pretend they are—smoky, noisy, giddy, dull, clumsy means of going from place to place," he said in a letter to Catherine Sedgwick. The train took an hour, and went only to Long Island City. From there, Bryant would have had to take a ferry. In the 1850's he often took a ferry instead from Glen Cove, and in later times, from a landing at the foot of his property at Cedarmere. The trip to Brooklyn took about three hours and from there Bryant would have had to reach New York by another steamboat, probably debarking at Whitehall Street or at Peck Slip in lower Manhattan.

Certainly the traveling was not a continuing pleasure, but, as it has become for countless commuters, it was a means to pleasure—a way to get away from the city into a more rural life and Bryant was not entirely averse to its hardships. One of his guests wrote about one trip on the steamer:

50

". . . We breakfasted early in order to take the steamer for New York. It was but a few moments' walk to the landing, but we descended a steep bluff or hill, and the house we had just left was lost to view. Mr. Bryant stopped to caress a little Scotch terrier as we hurried along, telling me at the same time the romantic story of the dog, which had once belonged to a Massachusetts stage-driver. We had almost reached the boat, when Mr. Bryant became aware that a beautiful little pet kitten was trotting proudly along beside us. 'Oh!' he exclaimed, 'you cannot go to New York.' Then, stooping, he gathered the not unwilling kitten into his arms and started on a run toward the house. I turned and looked after him, wondering if he would risk losing the boat by retracing the whole distance, and if there were many young men who would take so much trouble and display so much energy for a kitten! On he ran, up the sharp steep, never once pausing for breath or slackening his pace, and out of sight through the trees, depositing his burden in the house and closing the door. Then he ran all the way back to the steamer, less disconcerted apparently by the brisk exercise than half the schoolboys on the continent might have been . . . At Glen Cove, where the steamer stopped, Mr. Samuel L. M. Barlow came aboard, and chatted with Mr. Bryant about a remarkable tree they cultivate in North Holland—a sure preventative against malaria. Mr. Barlow had obtained some for himself and Mr. Bryant, and both gentlemen were experimenting on its culture in this climate . . ."

Even as a commuter, Bryant was vigorous and exuberant. The writer of the magazine article who had traveled with Bryant on the ferry trip, remembered his teasing comment on the way sunshine played over the "plain face of a young woman opposite which elongated her nose and shortened it according to the motion of the boat . . ." Even a dash for the ferry couldn't daunt one of the island's first commuters.

By lonely

walks where,

lovers stray

'Till the

Tender

stars appear?

FACSIMILE OF EDEN

LWAYS Bryant's letters were full of the activities at
Roslyn, and of its physical beauty. From his office in
New York he wrote to Mrs. Moulton, "Roslyn, meantime, is as beautiful as ever. It began to fade a little with
the drought, but the rains of the third and fourth of July
revived it. I have lengthened the walk in the woods so
that one can now pass over the greater part of them. All that now remains
to do is to put up seats and open areas by thinning or pruning the trees here
and there. You should be there, with your quick observation and accurate
taste, to tell where and how it should be done."

He made many such alterations. Some of the changes included removal of a heavy cornice and pillars that Mrs. Moulton's husband had added to the house, and substitution of lattice work, which afforded more light to the inside of the home and permitted the vines to twine. He realigned the road to the house which had formerly run alongside the inlet. Bryant remodelled it into a sweeping curve over the hilltop, furnishing, one writer said, "an uninterrupted slope from the house to the water-side and to afford an ample parterre for flowers, and winding walks, and bring the grapery into full view from the porch."

The writer had visited Bryant at Cedarmere after the poet had been away from home for several weeks, and he was charmed to witness the cordial welcome Bryant received. George Cline, the schoolmaster turned manager of Bryant's estate, "had become a sort of necessity in the household." Cline lived in a small refurbished cottage near the house. "The relations between the major domo and the poet are of the most agreeable and confidential kind. Each little detail about the farm management is discussed with the gravity and interest that those who reside in the country think due to such matters . . . (I) was much impressed with the kindly manner in which each of the household was greeted by him, showing the pleasant relations subsisting between a kind employer and attached employes.

"The little incidents of country gossip told by Mr. Cline were listened to with an interest by Bryant that showed how deeply he was interested in the concerns of the neighborhood, and how keenly he participated in all their joys and sorrows, and yet he has a reputation of being a reserved if not an austere man."

The seeds of his love for horticulture were planted early in life when he walked through the woods. He began early his long and detailed observations of nature, noticing when and where floral species began blooming and writing with sadness that he would not be at home when their blooming periods would begin.

Bryant tended the grounds at Cedarmere with the care and lavish affection that was his lifelong attitude toward things he loved—a puritanical orientation that demanded moral and ethical attention to each obligation. But there was more than duty in his tending of the land—in it he seemed to find both psychical and physical pleasure. In a lecture he delivered before the New York Horticultural Society, Bryant said,

"The earliest occupation of man, we are told—his task in the state of innocence, was to tend and dress the garden in which his maker placed him. I cannot say that as men addict themselves to the same pursuit they are raised nearer to the state of innocence, but this I will say; that few pursuits are so agreeably interesting without ever disturbing the mind, and that he who gives himself to it sets up one barrier more against evil thoughts and unhallowed wishes. The love of plants is a natural and wholesome instinct. Through that, perhaps, quite as much as through any other tendency of our natures, the sense of beauty, the grateful perception of harmony, of color, and of grace, and fair proportion of shape, enter the mind and wean it from grosser and more sensual tastes. The Quakers, who hesitate to cultivate some of the fine arts, indulge their love of beauty without scruple or restraint in rearing flowers and embellishing their grounds. I never read description of natural scenery nor expressions of delight at the beauty of vegetable products more enthusiastic than those in the travels of old Bartram the Quaker naturalist, recording his wanderings in Florida."

In another portion of the address, he said, "I have gathered roses in my garden on Long Island on the 20th of December. Last year I broke them from their stems on the 10th. It is curious to see the plant go on putting forth its flowers and raising its clusters of buds as if without any presentiment of approaching winter, till in the midst of bloom it is surprised by a frost nipping all its young and tender shoots at once, like a sudden failure overtaking one of our men of commerce in the midst of his many projects."

The variety and breadth of his horticultural interest was indicated in that address: he talked of gardening methods world-wide, mentioning grapes in China where they made no wine, and Japanese methods of cultivation.

Bryant's view of the garden as a microcosmic, perfect world is perhaps akin to no time more than today, when so many are disaffected by urban living. There would probably be a chorus of agreement to these words, written for his address before the New York Horticultural Society:

"You, my friends, who are the members of the Horticultural Society, are engaged in a good work—the work of cherishing the relations of acquaintanceship and affection too apt to be overlooked and forgotten in a city life, with the vegetable world in the midst of which God has placed us, and on which he made us so essentially dependent. So far as you occupy your minds with these natural and simple tastes, you keep yourselves unperverted by the world, and preserve in sight a reminiscence of the fair original garden."

Bryant lived by those words, occupying his leisure with natural and simple tastes, under the dictates of the puritanical values in which he'd been steeped in childhood and which remained with him to the end. And in the doing, he transformed Cedarmere into a facsimile of that "fair original garden."

Or
haply dost thou linger
On barren plains
and bare,
Or clamber the bald
mountain-side
Into the thinner air?—

THE POET

RYANT was as unique as a poet as he was in all other aspects of his life. He wrote in a new country, whose literature, due to a common literary heritage and common language with the mother country, England, followed the usual pattern of a transplanted literature to an indigenous one: borrowing, imitation, creation. But Bryant created from the beginning, and combined in his poetry elements from the various styles and

55

schools of literature—those which preceded him and those of his time—elements of Classicism, Romanticism and of Naturalism, along with strong traces of Calvinist patterns which shaped his early years.

Bryant's predecessors and contemporaries accomplished their works through a thicket of religious and political upheaval. These early artists were dealing with the concept of a God who brooked no creative rivalry. Due to an intense period of scientific discovery, they came to view the universe, natural and social, as divinely and precisely ordered down to its least inhabitant. Since all was as it should be in the world and since all new ideas came under the scrutiny of God's manifest word, the Bible, there was little difference in literary styles and few deviations. All art was predictable and ordered; form preceded content.

This satisfied an audience whose settlers were of only two kinds. They were either Puritans, religious outcasts who had quarreled with the Stuarts of England and whose leaders in America ruled them in all affairs, religious and social, or they were landed gentry, a leisured group of persons with gentle ideas who desired no art designed to stimulate or provoke.

As America moved towards the Revolution, new ideas infiltrated and a sense of rebelliousness and of national pride grew apace. But progress towards a new evaluation of the worth of the individual was difficult and uneven. The new literature had enemies on all sides. In a country rife with factionalism, fragmentation of purpose and a diversity of religious and national backgrounds, fads and new ideas gained favor quickly but were as quickly dispelled. There were influential American authors like James Fenimore Cooper, who, becoming suddenly conscious of the cultural crudity of his fellows, adulated and elevated all things English. He saw in democracy the death of history and of the old gentlemanly tradition. There were those who feared an intelligentsia, a literati, as a continuation of the old aristocratic social order. A further difficulty was the lack of publishers. Native authors paid for the publication of their own works and copyrights and stood the risk of sales. Publishers and book agents in various cities took their books on consignment. Furthermore, admiration for English literature was strong and publishers were apt to print only what was popular and a sure seller.

Possibly the strongest enemy of a native literature was democracy itself. One would think that a raw new country, settled by castoffs and a former aristocracy, would possess the material for a vital new literature, comprising the best of the past and the spirit and rebelliousness of the present. But nothing was permitted to interfere with the conduct of life in the new country and esthetics suffered at the hands of necessity. Literature that was apparent, easily apprehendable and entertaining was the literature that was popular. From the "vast, baccalaureate sermon" that Van Wyck Brooks described, literature became what DeToqueville called "a softness of mind and heart." It was all of a part, as Cooper put it, "wholesome, but scentless native plants." Sameness prevailed; there were few subtle distinctions in a literature faced with such stiff oppositions and undistinguished by a patina of age and history except in slavish imitations. For how do you achieve a democratic literature? Cut everyone off at the same height, and let no one be a cut above.

As America grew, so did a new wave of Romantic writers, influenced in part by English writers like Gray, Cowper, Burns, Byron, Wordsworth, DeFoe, Pope, Addison and Swift. Bryant was part of this new group. Some of his contemporaries were Cooper, Poe, Hawthorne, Melville, Whittier, Lowell, Longfellow, Holmes, Emerson, Thoreau and Whitman. Except for Whitman, whose work in large part was ignored or scorned by his generation, the art of these writers had one striking similarity. They wrote little out of their own experiences, creating instead an alternate world that was essentially unreal. Cooper wrote of the primitives, the Indians of North America, creating an existence for them that was idealized and false; Hawthorne turned back to America's beginnings, seeking the meaning of man's experience in his dealings with sin and guilt; Poe, whose real gift to literature was not realized until it had been transmitted through French artists and had furthered the Symbolist movement, created a fantastical world of necromancy in which the senses mingled and overcame sense. Emerson sought to instruct man in creating his own destiny, but in an ephemeral fashion, and the influence of his pupil, Thoreau, was felt more strongly in the Twentieth Century through his latterday disciples, Gandhi and King, than it was in his own day. Melville turned to the seas to construct his fantasies; Holmes wrote casual verse and Lowell criticism, both from their academic removes, while Longfellow turned to prehistory.

In this void of imitation and avoidance, Bryant stood out. He was determined that American literature could become a force to reckon with, that a literature could develop that would not ape the fashions of England. Aware that there was little motive and little reward for American writers, he urged them nonetheless to abandon servile copying and to praise literature according to intrinsic merit and not its geographic origin, since this would promote even further imitation of something already bad. Though writers still might find it necessary to seek patronage in England, he believed they could preserve their integrity.

"Abroad our literature has fallen under unmerited contumely from those who were but slenderly acquainted with the subject. . .but American authors must abandon pretentiousness which provokes ridicule. . .must produce better claim to fame than an 'extract from the parish register in order to preserve a pure taste' in both the readers and authors of America," he wrote.

Bryant's faith in his country's artists would not in itself assure him of a place of any honor or merit in a consideration of our literature. He has often been attacked and criticized as a moralist or as lacking in intellectual 57 depth or dismissed lightly as a "nature poet," and anthologies which claim to include America's major poets often contain not one of Bryant's poems. But Bryant cannot be so easily dismissed. He was a transitional poet and perhaps the only truly representational poet of worth between Philip Freneau and Edgar Allen Poe. Essentially a Romantic, he was ever conscious of the power of harmonious language, and of the importance of imagination and sentiment, yet he did not create picturesque beauty at the expense of form. Rather, he was equally concerned with preserving elegance and proportion, in maintaining a simplicity and clarity of thought and form. While there were didactic themes in his work and a sense that religious truth can be gained from observations in nature, this is more evidence of Naturalism than of moralism. Nature in Bryant's world is a place of renewal, of restoration, a stage on which endless, succeeding generations play their proper roles and give way to newer players. His detailed representations of things in life and in nature are without idealization. It is God's manifestations which teach, and not God's Biblical word, and in this Bryant's work is relieved of the aspersion of moralizing. If there are indefinite areas where these elements cross and sometimes conflict, this unevenness is found in the work of most artists. Bryant wrote in a new nation, in a new era, in one in which writing passed through vogues and vagaries as rough and as rowdy as itself, and his voice, in part due to his effectiveness as editor of The New York Evening Post, was influential for almost half a century.

Though Bryant may have longed to be a contemplative, his early habit of close examination of all aspects of his environment led him into a life of continuing examination and experimentation, and made him in fact a man of action, a productive man, a busy man. Sixty-four years elapsed between the writing of "Thanatopsis" and "The Flood of Years," and the quantity and scope of the work he produced in those years is prodigious. From the early contributions to the United States Literary Gazette and The Talisman, through the production, along with Washington Irving, of *The Tales of The Glauber Spa,* through the publication of various editions of his own poetry and his editings of the works of others, through the launchings of short-lived, small gazettes and journals, he labored tirelessly. Apart from his journalistic career, he delivered lectures and testimonials, discourses and odes, and contributed poetry, essays, biographical and nature sketches to still other publications. He wrote volumes on his travels to Scotland, Italy, France, Germany, Switzerland, the Orient and many other parts of the world. His work and his enthusiasm for it continued unabated through old age and throughout his lifetime he enjoyed high regard and respect.

His poetic career spanned six decades, and it was not his only career. These vocations, and avocations, along with all his questing interests, were bound to effect changes in point of view. It is fruitless to speculate on what he might have produced if he had devoted himself solely to poetry. It is sufficient that he produced a substantial body of poetry while engaged in broad service to his country. Bryant's poetry has long been overlooked and underestimated, but he would probably find satisfaction that, sharing the doom of mortality, he is resurrected in the eternal flow, one

"Whose part, in all the pomp that fills
The circuit of the summer hills,
Is that his grave is green."

Where
they who
journey upward
Walk in a
weary track,

CONCEPTS OF POETRY

BRYANT termed poetry the most venerable branch of literature and had distinct views on its creation. His lectures on poetry, widely acclaimed and closely attended, outlined his major premises and showed the various influences at work in his own poetry. They still provide an acceptable guide for the necessary ingredients of good poetry. Aware that poetry of one age and country differed widely from that of any other, and that there were many schools and followers of those schools—of varying capabili-

60

ties—he instructed poets to ignore fad and fashion and to seek universality.

Form is essential in poetry, and separates it from prose, Bryant believed. It was not enough for him that poetry be either vividly evocative or stimulative of strong feeling, nor that it produce wisdom in its reader. He believed firmly that poetry was a suggestive art, one which depended strongly on the use of symbols and demanded the reader's imagination and participation. But neither was it enough to create the jewel of an idea or a symbol. Setting was vital; a proper arrangement of beautiful flowers enhances their beauty.

Neither was it proper for a poet to use material which smacked even slightly of crudity or triviality. Something created for its shock value had no lasting value, in Bryant's estimation.

The third element which he believed separated poetry from prose was metrical harmony and precision of language. There was no accidental choice of word in a poem. All was carefully woven and rewoven. And no one was a greater exponent of his teachings than Bryant himself. He often wrote on scraps of paper, the backs of envelopes and manuscripts, and then transcribed what he had written to a clean sheet of paper, before sending it out. One such scrap shows an explanation of the word Thanatopsis:

". . . You ask the meaning of the word Thanatopsis. It is made up of two Greek words. Thanatos means death, any (aspect) of being, prospect light appearance I coined it when ~~little more than scarcely out of my boyhood~~ yet a mere boy."

This fragment, too, with its crossed out words, is on a piece of paper which contains thoughts for a poem:

"I will see thy praise (thru?) all the earth
A palace ~~full~~ *with* ~~health~~ flow uninhabited with good and
after give to wanderer . . . . where they might be
Whatever need ~~that came to me~~ sought me out
How many were my devils??
Of all the men (who?) live luxuriantly . . ."

If this seems utter nonsense, it is not, for Bryant did not write nonsense. He was a stickler for precision in all that he wrote and did. He constantly revised his own work, seeking the exact word to express the meaning he desired. This seemingly senseless bunch of phrases may have metamorphosed into a more concrete form or have been only jottings of an idea which never developed further. But the "careful poet" earned this sobriquet deservedly, revising his poems many times as they were published and reissued.

Bryant's further advice to poets was that they avoid striking novelty of expression or subtlety of thought which was far removed from common usage. He dismissed the metaphysical poets as a "class of wits" who practiced such elaborate conceits in their works that "one wonders how the mind of the author devised it." As he expressed it in *"The Poet,"* a poem is not a summer day's pastime, based on "empty gusts of passion." Only things of substance should be dealt with and then only after consideration. One should immerse oneself in the tumult and actively experience it, then detach from it in order to record it. This belief separated him distinctly from strict Romantic classification.

Poetry for Bryant, then, should appeal not only to and through the senses, but to the sense, with intellect controlling flow. And the poet was to sift and sift to eliminate the unnecessary, the uneven and the poor. "No one," said Bryant, "has an idea how much I reject of my own." There were, in fact, only 13,000 lines which he preserved, one third of it written before 1829, and all of those, he said (and his friends substantiated) he could recall at will, and word for word.

While emphasizing form and content, he was not indifferent to the fact that poetry was a synergistic relationship, a mutual enterprise through ages. In a first edition of a compilation of the best American and English literature which he edited, he stated in the preface:

"Poets are formed by their influence on one another . . . the greatest are indebted to their predecessors or contemporaries. The varieties of poetic excellence are as great as the varieties of beauty in flowers or in the female face."

Bryant's ideas on poetic construction differed too from those of his contemporaries. He averaged 75 lines in his own poems, believing that a long poem was "as impossible as a long ecstasy." He detested affectation. In writing to R. H. Dana about Cowper's translation of Homer, he protested Cowper's flowery translation as "such stilted phrase." He knew that English was a difficult language with which to effect satisfactory translation. He believed that literal translation was necessary to do justice to the original and that faithful translations should be done in blank verse, since the use of rhyme was "a constant temptation to petty infidelities" which led to the sacrifice of the work's dignity. He refused, almost without exception, to write "occasional" poetry—verse written for special occasions—calling it rarely worthy of its subject. It is likely that he often thought the subjects not worthy of poetry.

Bryant, also, departing from the prevailing view which held that America was too unformed to provide suitable themes for poetry, believed instead that there was boundless material in an untouched continent—sufficient for any artist's needs. He wanted America to throw off the British yoke, though, pragmatic, this neither prevented him from seeking publication of his own works in England, nor from advising others to do the same. Nor did he make light of the past and its teachings, knowing there was much to be gained from the long cultural history of Europe. He did not view scientific discovery in as dire a fashion as did Poe—"Vulture, whose wings are dull realities." If he saw the potential science had to limit and narrow imagination, he also saw the need for scientific progress and its inevitability. Culture reels in the wake of progress, but new discovery breeds new thought and new art.

Bryant's poetry is not nature poetry. Instead, his poetry is a study of man's ineluctable part in nature, of the inescapable lessons to be learned from nature, the "sermons in stones." Man is not a pawn. His destiny is his own choosing, as he is a necessary and harmonious element in the grand design of nature.

And
oft upon the
shady vale
With longing
eyes look
back?

ACCEPTANCE AND POETIC PROGRESS

RYANT drew praise early in his career, Henry Dana protesting to Philips of the North American Review that "Thanatopsis" could not have been written by anyone on this side of the Atlantic. Its publication brought erroneous acclaim to Bryant's father as the putative author, because it was his father who sent the poems out for publication. It was not surprising that the eloquent blank verse of "Thanatopsis" was thought to be

64

the work of a mature and accomplished poet. If Bryant could froth such forgettable lines as:

"No more the brumal tempest sheds
Its gathered stores in sleety shower
Nor yet the vernal season spreads
Its verdant mantle gemmed with flowers"

in true Romantic fashion, still he was redeemed by such poems as Thanatopsis:

". . . Yet a few days and thee
the all-beholding sun shall see no more
In all his course; nor yet in the cold ground,
Where thy pale form was laid, with many tears,
Nor in the embrace of ocean, shall exist
Thy image. Earth, that nourished thee, shall claim
Thy growth, to be resolved to earth again,
And, lost each human trace, surrendering up
Thine individual being, shalt thou go
To mix forever with the elements.
". . . The gay will laugh
When thou art gone, the solemn brood of care
Plod on, and each one as before will chase
His favorite phantom; yet all these shall leave
Their mirth and their employments, and shall come
And make their bed with thee. As the long train
Of ages glide away . . ."

And these lines from the perfect sonnet "Mutation":

"They talk of short-lived pleasure—be it so—
Pain dies as quickly; stern hard-featured pain
Expires and lets her weary prisoner go.
The fiercest agonies have shortest reign.
Weep not that the world changes—did it keep
A stable, changeless state, 'twere cause indeed to weep."

Like few other poets, living or dead, Bryant received not only continued acclaim from his contemporaries throughout his literary career, but also received a substantial return from his published editions of his poetry and from his lectures. He was called by Cooper "a poet of rare merit"; by Emerson "an original" who was as good as, if not better than, Milton, and a man who never sacrificed a principle nor was ever unfaithful to his convictions. Although he decried imitations, it was said of him that he had decided influences in his own poetry, particularly those of Wordsworth and the English "Graveyard Poets" such as Gray, Southey and Kirke White. But Richard Stoddard wrote in Appleton's Journal in 1871, ". . . Bryant has all the excellence of Wordsworth and none of his defects. His thought is as large and his language as imaginative; his heart is larger and his sympathies have a wider range."

Stoddard, as did Emerson, also praised his unrivalled descriptions of the beauties of the North American landscape. Poe criticized him for word usage, but praised him for the accuracy of his forms—some of which had been called awkward. Poe validated such forms by illustrating their past use by poets such as Pope and Milton. He too praised Bryant's moral vision and his descriptions of natural beauty.

Bryant also had earned a reputation in America and England as an astute critic, at an early stage of his career, with the essay he had written on Solyman Brown's book.

But Bryant himself was not so sure of his position or its worth. In 1832, he wrote to Dana ". . . poetry is an unprofitable trade, and I am very glad that I have something more certain to depend upon for a living." And again, in 1833: "After all, poetic wares are not in the market of the present day. Poetry may get praised in the newspapers but no man makes money by it, for the simple reason that nobody cares a fig for it. The taste for it is somewhat old-fashioned; the march of the age is in another direction— mankind are occupied with politics, railroads and steamboats. Hundreds will talk flippantly and volubly about poetry and even write about it who know no more of the matter and have no more feeling of poetry than the old stump I write this letter with."

Williams College President Mark Hopkins remarked later that they were indeed strange times (when) "poets not only possess money but patronize literature . . ." But Bryant had worked long and hard at many demanding projects before he attained a comfortable financial position. His first editorial position in the 1820's paid him $1,000, no great sum, as he admitted, but twice what he had made from his law practice. Before 1849, the New York Evening Post, which he strove mightily to improve and which he described to Fanny as "a sad dull thing" before he took over, had average profits of $10,000 a year. His yearly share was $4,000. By 1860, the New York Evening Post showed profits of $70,000 and if Bryant had deeper worries then, he was at least financially secure. But, no less for Bryant than any poet, it was fortunate that he did not have to depend on the sale of his books for a living. His editions usually sold well, faring better than those of Thoreau, whose work sold so poorly that he once said: "I have a library of 900 volumes, 700 of which I wrote myself."

But renumeration was small. Even Bryant's critically acclaimed translations of the Iliad and the Odyssey, done in the 1870's and encompassing some 32 volumes of work and a six-year period of his life, had paid only $17,451 to his estate in the ten years after his death. He would truly have been hard-pressed had he depended upon no other means of earning a living.

Bryant's biographers and critics often question whether Bryant would have been a better poet if he had devoted his considerable energies solely to poetry. It is true that his passion for poetry and for a writing career suffered fluctuations. Whether this was due to his own doubts as to his abilities as a poet or to the demands of finances and family responsibilities, we cannot be certain. The only question that need be answered is whether America, both in a literary and a social sense, profited or lost by the diversion of his powers to occupations other than poetry.

I hear
a solemn
murmur,
And listening to
the sound,

WAVERINGS

ALTHOUGH Bryant had received thorough and careful education at home, his higher education was endangered by strained family finances. He tried to keep his expenses small, asking his father in an embarrassed manner for his needs. "I have been obliged to speak for a pair of shoes. It does not require a longer time for my shoes to get their eyes open than it does a kitten." He longed to attend Yale, but, conscious of the family's straitened circumstances, he wrote to his friend Avery in a brief note that he was going to abandon schooling. "Who needs education, the bane of human existence . . . better to be a blacksmith . . .

(and read) sermons in stones . . ." But he was already aware that material interests were drawing him from his first passion, that of poetry, and feared its total dissipation. He expressed this passionately at this time in "I Cannot Forget With What Fervid Devotion."

"I cannot forget with what fervid devotion
I worshipped the visions of verse and of fame;
Each gaze at the glories of earth, sky and ocean,
To my kindled emotions, was wind over flame."
Bright visions! I mixed with the world and ye faded,
No longer your pure rural worshipper now;
In the haunts your continual presence pervaded,
Ye shrink from the signet of care on my brow.
Oh, leave not forlorn and forever forsaken,
Your pupil and victim to life and its tears!
But sometimes return, and in mercy awaken,
The glories ye showed to his earliest years."

And in another poem, "I Broke the Spell That Held Me Long," he discusses his attempt to pursue a practical career, one that would pay, and his inability to keep himself from his true interest.

"I broke the spell that held me long,
The dear, dear witchery of song.
I said the poet's idle lore
Shall waste my prime of years no more.
For Poetry, though heavenly born,
Consorts with poverty and scorn.
I broke the spell—nor deemed its power
Could fetter me another hour.
Ah, thoughtless! How could I forget,
Its causes were around me yet?
For wheresoe'er I looked, the while,
Was Nature's everlasting smile.
Still came and lingered on my sight
Of flowers and streams the bloom and light,
And glory of the stars and sun—
And these and poetry are one.
They, ere the world had held me long,
Recalled me to the love of song."

These poems not only disclose Bryant's doubts as to whether or not he still possessed his full poetic powers and his irreconcilable desire to pursue his art, but also illustrate a constant theme in his poetry: poetry and purity are inextricably mixed with elements of nature, and man, removed from harmony with the universe by worldly and material preoccupation, can be neither content nor productive. Bryant had wandered the regions of "desert and illimitable air" which were the pure realms of spirit, in his youth. He 69 did not want to leave it. Still, if necessity demanded his hand at another task, he had faith that the Power which led the Waterfowl would lead his "steps aright." Warned early by his uncle to beware of books which were unworthy and which absorbed his attention at the expense of sober study, he passed along the same advice to his sister: "Indolence inflicts seven devils of regret (with which you should) wrestle and subdue . . . (choose) works of amusement which do not command immoderate perusal . . ."

And if not working, he also suffered the pangs of conscience, writing to Baylies in 1818: "I suffered from ill health, Blue Devils and Laziness which pinioned my arms and withheld my fingers from my pen." And in a letter to his friend George Downes ". . . my hours of leisure have been poisoned by ill-health and depression of the spirits." Isolated in Great Barrington from educated companions and his chosen element, he wrote to his father: "There are not many here who suffer an excess of passion for books."

But despite conflicting desires, Bryant's strong character always led him to pursue his activities to the full. Just as he studied ancient languages until he developed fluency so he studied and practiced law, winning the respect of the townspeople and achieving the position of justice of the peace, and just so he committed himself to literature and then to journalism. Finally leaving the law altogether, he went to New York in 1823 where he had been offered a post as the editor of the New York Review. Although his feelings about the law had become definite, his feelings about journalism had not. To Dana he wrote, "I have given up my profession, which was a shabby one, and I am not altogether certain that I have got into a better one . . ." And later, he added, "My dislike for law was augmenting daily and my residence (in Great Barrington) had become quite disagreeable. It cost me pain and perplexity to live on friendly terms with my neighbors . . . If I starve, I will at least starve in peace."

But, Bryant, like many another artist, soon found to his dismay that a career in journalism was not synonymous with a writing career. It is one thing to devote all your energy and talent to developing a body of literature under the kind eye and lavish hand of a patron, and quite another to divide those energies between the exacting if rewarding job of editor and the even more taxing task of poet/writer. Besides, Bryant's nature made it imperative that he do both equally well. His complaints continued. To Dana, he wrote, "I am a draught horse . . . I would withdraw if I could. I am growing more discontented and impatient at my lot." And to his brother in Illinois (when his assistant editor at the New York Evening Post, Leggett, was ill), he said, "I have no leisure for poetry."

Nevertheless, Bryant continued in his editorial position for 50 years. It is not inconceivable that doubts sometimes nagged him about flagging poetic powers because he was so far removed from those soothing aspects of nature which he believed were necessary to man's spiritual well being

and the contemplative state which precedes the creation of poetry. Still he was a practical man. Determined, pragmatic, he accepted responsibilities which were thrust upon him or which he freely chose.

He was not doctrinaire in his beliefs. A staunch churchgoer, reared in Calvinist tradition, he nonetheless changed his affiliation first to Baptist and then to Unitarian as his religious thought grew and broadened and as different pastors' ideas and sermons appealed to his changing inner convictions. He was broad-minded, yet firm enough to adjust his political and social beliefs in accordance with the changing world and his own unwavering conscience. Nevertheless he kept those beliefs above and apart from popular stances or outside influence. He refused, as noted, to attend political affairs or social functions where his influence might be solicited or his newspaper might be compromised. He preferred to maintain his detachment from political tentacles even to the point of refusing to visit Washington. "I was there once," he said.

If his temper could flare violently, he could also repent and forgive, revising his opinions if, after consideration, he felt that they had been unjust. A moral man, he was offended by some of what he considered to be the libertine views of Whitman, but that did not prevent Bryant from affirming Whitman's power as a poet, nor from proving a gracious host to the younger poet. In fact, Bryant was personally charmed by Whitman, and as he conducted his political and journalistic affairs he also conducted his literary and personal affairs, maintaining an open attitude to new ideas but never departing from his own ethical standards. And his own poetry, developing its main thrust slowly from his first real poem, "Thanatopsis," never lost sight of those high standards.

I know
the
voice of the
mighty sea,
Beating his pebbly bound

IN PRAISE OF LIFE

F THE composition date of "Thanatopsis" is uncertain, its merit is not. Its incomparable blank verse, its fluid language and power of thought made an auspicious beginning for the young poet which was difficult to surpass. It was not easy to ignore the types of prevalent poetry which were popular and successful and still to maintain the sweep and elegance evident in "Thanatopsis."

There is undoubtedly unevenness in Bryant's poetry. He struggled with his youthful passions, his lingering regard for the morbid tone of the

72

Graveyard Poets of England and of the German Romanticists. These gloomy echoes of death and despair were considered by many, including Edgar Allen Poe, to be the fitting elements of a good poem. But from the beginning, Bryant's main theme is evident: the progress of life, and of death, is a progress of renewal, infinite and eternal.

Thus, from the earliest of his poems, "Thanatopsis," in which that which springs from earth is resolved to earth again to mingle forever with its atoms, Bryant presents his theme. In "The Burial Place," there is at first seeming praise for the old customs of England, where graves are bedecked with appropriate flowers: modest roses for virgins, primroses and pansies for babes, rue and rosemary for lovers. But the customs are not followed in raw new America; instead coarse grass sprouts between naked stones and nature alone plants the brier rose to soften the graves. Bryant's symbolism here extends further than nature's attempt at renewal. He is commenting on the growth of strong new nations, men and ideas, out of the feeble mould of old custom and dying lands. The new land grows fruit from its graves instead of dying flowers, grows ruddy strawberries that only the faint of heart would fear to grasp.

There were many lapses in Bryant's development of a unified theme, and it is difficult to explain the unevennesses even when popular themes and sheer quantity are taken into consideration. "The Yellow Violet," popular in his day, was moralizing, sentimental and romantic, with awkward construction and even more awkward analogy. Yet in "To A Waterfowl," with its crisp words and precise construction, written only a year later, Bryant was able to lift himself from "the warble and the beechen bud" of the earlier poem to the "desert and illimitable air . . . the cold, thin atmosphere" and strict form of the latter. And he continued his main theme in the second, reiterating his certain knowledge that there was an ordered progression for man as well as for the creatures of nature:

"He who, from zone to zone,
Guides through the boundless sky thy certain flight
In the long way that I must tread alone,
Will lead my steps aright."

Bryant could write in "The Ages" thirty-five impeccable Spenserian stanzas. If one quarreled with superfluity of detail, the thought behind it or the flow of it, one could not deny the perfection of form. And if objections are raised to the unabashed Romanticism of "Oh, Fairest of the Rural Maids" written for Fanny, it must be remembered that Bryant was in the throes of his first real passion and that the form he chose did not deviate from what was then considered fitting tribute to virginal love. The beloved was always without sin and removed from the crudities of the real world. Her eyes could be no less than limpid pools or springs and her feet could not touch earth. He may also be forgiven "The West Wind" with its bright 73

June roses rising to its kiss, if only for the tinge of irony in its last stanza.

Bryant was casting about and choosing forms for his more mature thought to take. His "Hymn to Death" which begins as an attempt to reconcile Death as the avenger and adjuster of Life's ills is brought up short in the middle. Bryant at that time had experienced cruel loss of his own and became aware that much of his sermonizing was empty. It was a long progression through his work to his more considered view of death as an interstice, as one more step in an eternal progression.

It was fashionable for poets to do thematic pieces, to express in purer language, in loftier phrase, the thoughts and utterances of baser men. It was also fashionable to do set pieces, archaica, to write of prehistory and of the Noble Savage. "The Damsel of Peru," "The African Chief," "To A Cloud," "November," "After a Tempest" and the poor palliative "Blessed Are They That Mourn" are some of the pieces that Bryant wrote in this fashion. The poem "Song" below, incomplete here, is Bryant's equivalent of Herrick's advice to "The Virgins, To Make Much of Time," Jonson's "Song" to Celia and Andrew Marvell's "To His Coy Mistress":

"Dost thou idly ask to hear
At what gentle seasons
Nymphs relent, when lovers near
Press the tenderest reasons?
Ah! they give their faith too oft
To the careless wooer.
Maidens' hearts are always soft.
Would that men's were truer.
Let the scene, that tells how fast
Youth is passing over,
Warn her, ere her bloom is past,
To secure her lover."

At the same time, Bryant wrote poems such as "Lines on Revisiting the Country," "The Rivulet," "The Snow-Shower" and "A Forest Hymn." In varying degree they are illustrative of his main thought. In his exquisite blank verse, which he seemed to reserve for the expression of his deepest emotion, Bryant describes renewal in "A Forest Hymn":

"Lo! all grow old and die, but see again,
How on the faltering footsteps of decay
Youth presses—ever gay and beautiful
In all its beautiful forms. These lofty trees
Wave not less proudly that their ancestors
Moulder beneath them. Oh, there is not lost
One of earth's charms. Upon her bosom yet,
After the flight of untold centuries,
The freshness of her far beginning lies
And yet shall lie . . ."

And he senses that he also, like holy men who have sequestered themselves in forests, may restore himself:

> "Let me . . .
> Retire, and in thy presence reassure
> My feeble virtue. Here, its enemies,
> The passions, at thy plainer footsteps shrink
> And tremble and are still."

Life, in the groves that are "God's first temples," sits and renews itself on Death's very sepulchre. Far from the impure structures which man builds and in which he presumes to worship God, there are no echoes of man's evils of pride and pomp. There are instead, "Simples" or healing plants beside the banks of healing waters, givers of grace and strength. There is "calm society" while man is at peace with his conscience and his world, in harmony with the harmoniousness of nature. Once turned back to "the haunts of men . . . the ills of life . . ." there, man loses repose as rivers lose their repose to the moon-ordered tides, and is prey to the things that make him loathe his life.

But it is not simply that nature restores. Man is instrumental in ordering his life and his world about him. He suffers dire consequences only if he is destructive of "the beautiful order" of God's works in nature or if he refuses to conform the order of his life to the order apparent in nature. Man is transient, and walks on tombs, but while he continues in harmony, he is at peace, he is allotted a portion, a taste of the grandeur that in "Scene on the Banks of the Hudson" is described as "too much of Heaven on earth to last." Though his works on earth are mere "proud piles," man's faltering footsteps on "The Journey of Life" are still guided by certain Hands to "boundless light."

The theme of renewal continues in "The Song of The Sower", the atoms of individual being mingle with the elements of earth and air:

> ". . . we fling
> o'er the dark mould the green of spring . . .
> . . . we trust the strength of armies to the dust"
>   and
> "Out of heaven's unmeasured blue
> Shall walk again the genial year
> To wake with warmth and nurse with dew
> The germs we lay to slumber here."

Man buries his past and plants his future, trusting and believing in rebirth. And nature's atoms, her

> "airs, whose breathing stirs,
> The fresh grass, are our fellow worshippers."

For Bryant did not separate man from his universe. In "Sella," apparently 75 a fairy tale, a human girl is made divine by the element of water. Forced by her family to return to the harsh and killing upper world, she turns to God and acts of mercy in His world and by this is reconciled to earth. She is granted the gift of dowsing and is able to bring forth for man the healing fountains and watersheds for mankind. In "The Return of the Birds" and "My Autumn Walk," birds flee before the armies of men bent on destruction. But nature mocks man's brief and temporal power. She claims the dead and restores herself by hanging her own "blood-red banner" of mock-grape in the bloodied fields. And in autumn

> "The leaves are swept from the branches;
> But the living buds are there
> With folded flower and foliage
> To sprout in a kinder air."

Nature will renew earth and the race of men which wrought the havoc.

What is most important about Bryant's work is that he wrote in praise of life even in the poems which seem most to deal with death. The "polestar" is fixed, despite our latterday knowledge, and does not alter with the "dances of that glittering train below" which is man's world. It remains the beacon by which we shape our lives. Those who die go only when the time is fitting, as in "The Old Man's Funeral:"

> "Ye sigh not when the sun, his course fulfilled,
> His glorious course, rejoicing earth and sky,
> In the soft evening, when the winds are stilled,
> Sinks where his islands of refreshment lie,
> And leaves the smile of his departure spread . . .
> "Why weep ye then for him, who, having won
> The bound of man's appointed years, at last,
> Life's blessings all enjoyed, life's labors done,
> Serenely to his final rest has passed?
> "Nor can I deem that Nature did him wrong,
> Softly to disengage the vital cord.
> For when his hand grew palsied, and his eye
> Dark with the mists of age, it was his time to die."

And the dead are with us:

> ". . . are here—they are here . . .
> In the yellow sunshine and flowing air
> In the light cloud shadows that slowly pass
> In the sounds that rise from the murmuring grass."

Since man was integral to nature and death to life, there was in Bryant's mature thought no fear of death as separation. His poem for Fanny, his wife of 45 years, written after her long illness and death, is keen with anguish at her loss:

> "I gaze in sadness,; it delights me not
> To look on beauty which thou canst not see;
> And, wert thou by my side, the dreariest spot
> Were, oh! how far more beautiful to me."

and though in "The Life That Is" he had fervently welcomed her back from the verge of death on which she had so long lingered and which he had so deeply feared, he continues in "October 1866:

> "May we not think that near us thou dost stand
> With loving ministrations, for we know
> Thy heart was never happy when thy hand
> Was forced its tasks of mercy to forego!"

Fanny remains close, even in death, and the month of October, even without her physical presence, is sweet and warm. Long Island Sound is blue and dotted with sails. Many late flowers abound with which to strew her grave. And though there is anguish in the hearts of her family and friends, there is also certainty that she remains. His own anticipated burial place in the poem "June" is a joyous spot. And the words with which he describes his certain death are joyous also: glorious, pleasant, rich, green, blue, golden, cheerful, lovely, brightness, wild music. There is no fear; the thought of coffin and mould are pushed away and he is content that his part of all the gladness of the scene, in all that passes in the lives of men, is that he has lived well in that he is now part of the green earth and that he too will be loved and missed.

Dost thou,
oh path of the
woodland!
End where
those
waters roar,

NOTHING TO DECAY

RYANT continued to write till shortly before his death. He deprecated what he considered his small output but suggested that had he written more it might not have been so well accepted. When he was feted at Williams College on his 70th birthday, he stated: "I am congratulated on having completed my 70th year. Is there nothing ambiguous in such a compliment? To be congratulated on one's senility! To be congratulated on having reached the stage of life when the bodily and mental powers pass into decline and decay." But he was far from senility and at the age of 76 began the translation of *The Odyssey*, exhorting the printer that there was no need to push him to work harder since he was well aware that jobs begun late in life were apt "to be brought to a conclusion before they are finished." As it was, he continued with *The Iliad,* finishing it in 1878, and warned the publishers: "Do not let your printers tread on my heels. It is disagreeable to be dunned for copy and I cannot write as well when I have any vexation of that sort on my mind." His able translations were, along with "The Flood of Years," almost the last things from his pen. And in "The Flood of Years" he sums up the thrust of his early poems:

"A mighty Hand, from an exhaustless Urn
Pours forth the never-ending Flood of Years.
. . . How the rushing waves
Bear all before them . . . Life, The Present . . .
The silent ocean of the Past . . . What is there beyond?
. . . bright river, broadening like a sea (that brings)
A Present in whose reign no grief shall gnaw
The heart, and never shall a tender tie
Be broken; in whose reign the eternal Change
That waits on growth and action shall proceed . . ."

Bryant was criticized by William Aspinwall Bradley as "lacking in intellectual depth" and praised by him for "accuracy of detail, an artistic gift of imagination and a genius for perfection." He was described by Nathanial Hawthorne as "easily conversant, but uttering neither passion nor poetry." He has been called old-fashioned, cozy and isolated, praised as having "the steady hand of a master and technical maturity." He has been ignored and denied a place in anthologies of American literature time after time. Perhaps it is time for a thorough re-evaluation of the wide contributions of this poet of whom the Reverend Dr. Henry Bellows, minister of All Souls Church which Bryant attended said:

"There is nothing to decay in his work: no careless phrases, no fashion of passing thought or utterance, no extravagances, no sentimentalism and no sing-song music."

Like human life, on a trackless beach With a boundless Sea before.

HYMNS FOR THE MINSTREL

S BRYANT neared the end of his life, he paid minor obeisances to aging, despite observations by others that he seemed as agile and young as persons many years his junior. He wrote to the Reverend Dewey, as death approached,

"I do not know how it may be with you, but for my part I feel an antipathy to hard work growing upon me. This morning I have been laboriously employed upon the Evening Post, and do not like it. Did you ever feel a sense of satiety—a feeling like that of an uncomfortably overloaded stomach—at the prospect of too much to do? Does the love of ease take possession of us as we approach the period when we must bid the world good night, just as we are predisposed to rest when evening comes?"

In the poem called "June" written many years before his death, Bryant had said he would choose that month above all to be laid to rest. On May 29, 1878, at the age of 84, Bryant spent a morning at his editorial chores in The New York Evening Post office, had his luncheon, and then traveled to Central Park to make a speech at the dedication of a statue to the Italian patriot Mazzini. It was a hot, sunny day, and the poet sat hatless on the dais, and seemed to shake, and lose his place several times during his speech, an unusual occurrence for the assured, self-confident speaker. The ceremonies over, he walked with his friend, James Grant Wilson to Wilson's home on Fifth Avenue, refusing to ride and also refusing to cover his head. As Wilson put the key in the lock he heard a crash behind him and turned to find that Bryant had fallen on the doorstep, injuring his head. Bryant was taken to his New York City home at West 16th Street by coach, where his daughter Julia and niece nursed him for two weeks.

He never really recovered full consciousness. On the 12th of June, 1878, he died.

New York's mayor ordered the flags of the city to be flown at half mast, and in the custom of the period, photographs of the poet-editor, with funerary drapings, were hung in many city windows. The city mourned one of its foremost citizens as it might have mourned an elected official.

Bryant was a private man, who would have been astonished had he been present at his own funeral. He had asked to have it conducted simply and unostentatiously. But the Reverend Dr. Bellows, pastor of the Church of All Souls, one of two Unitarian churches in Manhattan, had been a longtime friend of Bryant's, and Bryant had joined the pastor's congregation. Dr. Bellows persuaded his daughter Julia, against her will, to agree to a public service at All Souls, because Bryant had been so "public" a man. The crowds who appeared to pay homage to Bryant were so thick that police could not clear a path for the coffin, and had to force their way through the throngs.

Dr. Bellows delivered two funeral orations for his friend; the one at All Souls was followed by a graveside ceremony at Roslyn, next to the grave of his dear wife Fanny. Bryant's body was borne home to his Roslyn for the last time aboard a special private train, hired by his family from the Long Island Railroad.

He was buried on a day James Grant Wilson later recalled as "indeed glorious . . . the daisies were dancing and glimmering over the fields as the poet's family, a few old friends, and the villagers saw him laid in his last resting place at Roslyn after a few words fitly spoken by his pastor, and beheld his coffin, covered with roses and other summer flowers by a little grave. This act completed, we left the aged minstrel amid the melody dearest of all to him in life—the music of the gentle June breezes murmuring through the tree tops, from whence also came the songs of the summer birds."

Bryant, the public man who yet maintained his privacy, might still have understood the dichotomy between the two ceremonies that marked his passing—the well-attended ceremony at All Souls, and the quieter ceremony in Roslyn attended by his close friends and family, at the cemetery. He surely would have preferred the graveside ceremony in which the children of the village, who had so often visited him at Cedarmere for strawberry festivals, strewed flowers on his casket after it was lowered into the grave—to the sacred music, the sermon and the elaborate flowery tribute from "his employees who loved him"—at the church. The monument he erected for Fanny guards the graves of the Bryants. It seems a pity that the moss roses and woods violets he most loved could not be persuaded to grow on the plot in Roslyn Cemetery, but at least his beloved trees shade the graves.

A ROSLYN SAMPLER

Bryant once was described as "the poet for those who think while they feel." In no other form of writing, perhaps, is there so personal a confrontation between the author and his art as in poetry. Because it was the form he most loved, because his poetry has been neglected in anthologies, and because his mastery of form, technique, and content deserve a new appraisal, 20 of his poems are included in this "sampler."

Said to have been written in Roslyn, these poems are also representative of his many moods and styles, and the subjects with which his questing ranging, restless mind wrested.

We hope the selection will induce the new reader of Bryant to look further at his art.

THE May sun sheds an amber light
  On new-leaved woods and lawns between ;
But she who, with a smile more bright,
  Welcomed and watched the springing green,
      Is in her grave,
      Low in her grave.

The fair white blossoms of the wood
  In groups beside the pathway stand ;
But one, the gentle and the good,
  Who cropped them with a fairer hand,
      Is in her grave,
      Low in her grave.

Upon the woodland's morning airs
  The small birds' mingled notes are flung ;
But she, whose voice, more sweet than theirs,
  Once bade me listen while they sung,
      Is in her grave,
      Low in her grave.

That music of the early year
  Brings tears of anguish to my eyes ;
My heart aches when the flowers appear ;
  For then I think of her who lies
      Within her grave,
      Low in her grave.

THE VOICE OF AUTUMN.

THERE comes, from yonder height,
  A soft repining sound,
Where forest-leaves are bright,
And fall, like flakes of light,
      To the ground.

It is the autumn breeze,
 That, lightly floating on,
Just skims the weedy leas,
Just stirs the glowing trees,
  And is gone.

He moans by sedgy brook,
 And visits, with a sigh,
The last pale flowers that look,
From out their sunny nook,
  At the sky.

O'er shouting children flies
 That light October wind,
And, kissing cheeks and eyes,
He leaves their merry cries
  Far behind,

And wanders on to make
 That soft uneasy sound
By distant wood and lake,
Where distant fountains break
  From the ground.

No bower where maidens dwell
 Can win a moment's stay ;
Nor fair untrodden dell ;
He sweeps the upland swell,
  And away !

Mourn'st thou thy homeless state ?
 O soft, repining wind !
That early seek'st and late
The rest it is thy fate
  Not to find.

Not on the mountain's breast,
 Not on the ocean's shore,
In all the East and West :
The wind that stops to rest
  Is no more.

By valleys, woods, and springs,
　　No wonder thou shouldst grieve
For all the glorious things
Thou touchest with thy wings
　　　　　And must leave.

THE PLANTING OF THE APPLE-TREE.

COME, let us plant the apple-tree.
Cleave the tough greensward with the spade :
Wide let its hollow bed be made ;
There gently lay the roots, and there
Sift the dark mould with kindly care,
　　And press it o'er them tenderly,
As, round the sleeping infant's feet,
We softly fold the cradle-sheet ;
　　So plant we the apple-tree.

　　What plant we in this apple-tree?
Buds, which the breath of summer days
Shall lengthen into leafy sprays ;
Boughs where the thrush, with crimson breast,
Shall haunt and sing and hide her nest ;
　　We plant, upon the sunny lea,
A shadow for the noontide hour,
A shelter from the summer shower,
　　When we plant the apple-tree.

　　What plant we in this apple-tree?
Sweets for a hundred flowery springs
To load the May-wind's restless wings,
When, from the orchard-row, he pours
Its fragrance through our open doors ;
　　A world of blossoms for the bee,
Flowers for the sick girl's silent room,
For the glad infant sprigs of bloom,
　　We plant with the apple-tree.

What plant we in this apple-tree?
Fruits that shall swell in sunny June,
And redden in the August noon,
And drop, when gentle airs come by,
That fan the blue September sky,
   While children come, with cries of glee,
And seek them where the fragrant grass
Betrays their bed to those who pass,
   At the foot of the apple-tree.

And when, above this apple-tree,
The winter stars are quivering bright,
And winds go howling through the night,
Girls, whose young eyes o'erflow with mirth,
Shall peel its fruit by cottage-hearth,
   And guests in prouder homes shall see,
Heaped with the grape of Cintra's vine
And golden orange of the line,
   The fruit of the apple-tree.

The fruitage of this apple-tree
Winds and our flag of stripe and star
Shall bear to coasts that lie afar,
Where men shall wonder at the view,
And ask in what fair groves they grew;
   And sojourners beyond the sea
Shall think of childhood's careless day,
And long, long hours of summer play,
   In the shade of the apple-tree.

Each year shall give this apple-tree
A broader flush of roseate bloom,
A deeper maze of verdurous gloom,
And loosen, when the frost-clouds lower,
The crisp brown leaves in thicker shower.
   The years shall come and pass, but we
Shall hear no longer, where we lie,
The summer's songs, the autumn's sigh,
   In the boughs of the apple-tree.

And time shall waste this apple-tree.
Oh, when its aged branches throw
Thin shadows on the ground below,
Shall fraud and force and iron will
Oppress the weak and helpless still?
What shall the tasks of mercy be,
Amid the toils, the strifes, the tears
Of those who live when length of years
Is wasting this little apple-tree?

"Who planted this old apple-tree?"
The children of that distant day
Thus to some aged man shall say;
And, gazing on its mossy stem,
The gray-haired man shall answer them:
"A poet of the land was he,
Born in the rude but good old times;
'Tis said he made some quaint old rhymes,
On planting the apple-tree."

"No pampered bloom of the greenhouse chamber
Has half the charm of the lawn's first flower."

William Cullen Bryant

Roslyn, Long Island, October 3d. 1877.

Part of a poem written in Bryant's own handwriting

THE SNOW-SHOWER.

STAND here by my side and turn, I pray,
   On the lake below thy gentle eyes ;
The clouds hang over it, heavy and gray,
   And dark and silent the water lies ;
And out of that frozen mist the snow
In wavering flakes begins to flow ;
        Flake after flake
They sink in the dark and silent lake.

See how in a living swarm they come
   From the chambers beyond that misty veil ;
Some hover awhile in air, and some
   Rush prone from the sky like summer hail.
All, dropping swiftly or settling slow,
Meet, and are still in the depths below ;
        Flake after flake
Dissolved in the dark and silent lake.

Here delicate snow-stars, out of the cloud,
   Come floating downward in airy play,
Like spangles dropped from the glistening crowd
   That whiten by night the milky way ;
There broader and burlier masses fall ;
The sullen water buries them all—
        Flake after flake— ·
All drowned in the dark and silent lake.

And some, as on tender wings they glide
   From their chilly birth-cloud, dim and gray,
Are joined in their fall, and, side by side,
   Come clinging along their unsteady way ;
As friend with friend, or husband with wife,
Makes hand in hand the passage of life ;
        Each mated flake
Soon sinks in the dark and silent lake.

Lo ! while we are gazing, in swifter haste
   Stream down the snows, till the air is white,
As, myriads by myriads madly chased,
   They fling themselves from their shadowy height
The fair, frail creatures of middle sky,
What speed they make, with their grave so nigh ;
       Flake after flake,
To lie in the dark and silent lake !

I see in thy gentle eyes a tear ;
   They turn to me in sorrowful thought ;
Thou thinkest of friends, the good and dear,
   Who were for a time, and now are not ;
Like these fair children of cloud and frost,
That glisten a moment and then are lost,
       Flake after flake—
All lost in the dark and silent lake.

Yet look again, for the clouds divide ;
   A gleam of blue on the water lies ;
And far away, on the mountain-side,
   A sunbeam falls from the opening skies,
But the hurrying host that flew between
The cloud and the water, no more is seen ;
       Flake after flake,
At rest in the dark and silent lake.

A RAIN-DREAM.

THESE strifes, these tumults of the noisy world,
Where Fraud, the coward, tracks his prey by stealth,
And Strength, the ruffian, glories in his guilt,
Oppress the heart with sadness. Oh, my friend,
In what serener mood we look upon
The gloomiest aspects of the elements
Among the woods and fields ! Let us awhile,
As the slow wind is rolling up the storm,
In fancy leave this maze of dusty streets,

Forever shaken by the importunate jar
Of commerce, and upon the darkening air
Look from the shelter of our rural home.

Who is not awed that listens to the Rain,
Sending his voice before him ?   Mighty Rain !
The upland steeps are shrouded by thy mists ;
Thy shadow fills the hollow vale ; the pools
No longer glimmer, and the silvery streams
Darken to veins of lead at thy approach.
O mighty Rain ! already thou art here ;
And every roof is beaten by thy streams,
And, as thou passest, every glassy spring
Grows rough, and every leaf in all the woods
Is struck, and quivers.   All the hill-tops slake
Their thirst from thee ; a thousand languishing fields,
A thousand fainting gardens, are refreshed ;
A thousand idle rivulets start to speed,
And with the graver murmur of the storm
Blend their light voices as they hurry on.

Thou fill'st the circle of the atmosphere
Alone ; there is no living thing abroad,
No bird to wing the air nor beast to walk
The field ; the squirrel in the forest seeks
His hollow tree ; the marmot of the field
Has scampered to his den ; the butterfly
Hides under her broad leaf ; the insect crowds,
That made the sunshine populous, lie close
In their mysterious shelters, whence the sun
Will summon them again.   The mighty Rain
Holds the vast empire of the sky alone.

I shut my eyes, and see, as in a dream,
The friendly clouds drop down spring violets
And summer columbines, and all the flowers
That tuft the woodland floor, or overarch
The streamlet :—spiky grass for genial June,
Brown harvests for the waiting husbandman,
And for the woods a deluge of fresh leaves.

I see these myriad drops that slake the dust,
Gathered in glorious streams, or rolling blue

In billows on the lake or on the deep,
And bearing navies.   I behold them change
To threads of crystal as they sink in earth
And leave its stains behind, to rise again
In pleasant nooks of verdure, where the child,
Thirsty with play, in both his little hands
Shall take the cool, clear water, raising it
To wet his pretty lips.   To-morrow noon
How proudly will the water-lily ride
The brimming pool, o'erlooking, like a queen,
Her circle of broad leaves !   In lonely wastes,
When next the sunshine makes them beautiful,
Gay troops of butterflies shall light to drink
At the replenished hollows of the rock.

Now slowly falls the dull blank night, and still,
All through the starless hours, the mighty Rain
Smites with perpetual sound the forest-leaves,
And beats the matted grass, and still the earth
Drinks the unstinted bounty of the clouds—
Drinks for her cottage wells, her woodland brooks—
Drinks for the springing trout, the toiling bee,
And brooding bird—drinks for her tender flowers,
Tall oaks, and all the herbage of her hills.

A melancholy sound is in the air,
A deep sigh in the distance, a shrill wail
Around my dwelling.   'Tis the Wind of night ;
A lonely wanderer between earth and cloud,
In the black shadow and the chilly mist,
Along the streaming mountain-side, and through
The dripping woods, and o'er the plashy fields,
Roaming and sorrowing still, like one who makes
The journey of life alone, and nowhere meets
A welcome or a friend, and still goes on
In darkness.   Yet a while, a little while,
And he shall toss the glittering leaves in play,
And dally with the flowers, and gayly lift
The slender herbs, pressed low by weight of rain,
And drive, in joyous triumph, through the sky,
White clouds, the laggard remnants of the storm.

ROBERT OF LINCOLN.

MERRILY swinging on brier and weed,
  Near to the nest of his little dame,
Over the mountain-side or mead,
  Robert of Lincoln is telling his name :
      Bob-o'-link, bob-o'-link,
      Spink, spank, spink ;
Snug and safe is that nest of ours,
Hidden among the summer flowers.
            Chee, chee, chee.

Robert of Lincoln is gayly drest,
  Wearing a bright black wedding-coat ;
White are his shoulders and white his crest.
  Hear him call in his merry note :
      Bob-o'-link, bob-o'-link,
      Spink, spank, spink ;
Look, what a nice new coat is mine,
Sure there was never a bird so fine.
            Chee, chee, chee.

Robert of Lincoln's Quaker wife,
  Pretty and quiet, with plain brown wings,
Passing at home a patient life,
  Broods in the grass while her husband sings :
      Bob-o'-link, bob-o'-link,
      Spink, spank, spink ;
Brood, kind creature ; you need not fear
Thieves and robbers while I am here.
            Chee, chee, chee.

Modest and shy as a nun is she ;
  One weak chirp is her only note.
Braggart and prince of braggarts is he,
  Pouring boasts from his little throat :
      Bob-o'-link, bob-o'-link,
      Spink, spank, spink ;

Never was I afraid of man ;
Catch me, cowardly knaves, if you can !
        Chee, chee, chee.

Six white eggs on a bed of hay,
  Flecked with purple, a pretty sight !
There as the mother sits all day,
  Robert is singing with all his might :
    Bob-o'-link, bob-o'-link,
    Spink, spank, spink ;
Nice good wife, that never goes out,
Keeping house while I frolic about.
        Chee, chee, chee.

Soon as the little ones chip the shell,
  Six wide mouths are open for food ;
Robert of Lincoln bestirs him well,
  Gathering seeds for the hungry brood.
    Bob-o'-link, bob-o'-link,
    Spink, spank, spink ;
This new life is likely to be
Hard for a gay young fellow like me.
        Chee, chee, chee.

Robert of Lincoln at length is made
  Sober with work, and silent with care ;
Off is his holiday garment laid,
  Half forgotten that merry air :
    Bob-o'-link, bob-o'-link,
    Spink, spank, spink ;
Nobody knows but my mate and I
Where our nest and our nestlings lie.
        Chee, chee, chee.

Summer wanes ; the children are grown ;
  Fun and frolic no more he knows ;
Robert of Lincoln's a humdrum crone ;
  Off he flies, and we sing as he goes :
    Bob-o'-link, bob-o'-link,
    Spink, spank, spink ;

When you can pipe that merry old strain,
Robert of Lincoln, come back again.
        Chee, chee, chee.

THE TWENTY–SEVENTH OF MARCH.

OH, gentle one, thy birthday sun should rise
Amid a chorus of the merriest birds
That ever sang the stars out of the sky
In a June morning.   Rivulets should send
A voice of gladness from their winding paths,
Deep in o'erarching grass, where playful winds,
Stirring the loaded stems, should shower the dew
Upon the grassy water.   Newly-blown
Roses, by thousands, to the garden-walks
Should tempt the loitering moth and diligent bee.
The longest, brightest day in all the year
Should be the day on which thy cheerful eyes
First opened on the earth, to make thy haunts
Fairer and gladder for thy kindly looks.
    Thus might a poet say ; but I must bring
A birthday offering of an humbler strain,
And yet it may not please thee less.   I hold
That 'twas the fitting season for thy birth
When March, just ready to depart, begins
To soften into April.   Then we have
The delicatest and most welcome flowers,
And yet they take least heed of bitter wind
And lowering sky.   The periwinkle then,
In an hour's sunshine, lifts her azure blooms
Beside the cottage-door ; within the woods
Tufts of ground-laurel, creeping underneath
The leaves of the last summer, send their sweets
Up to the chilly air, and, by the oak,
The squirrel-cups, a graceful company,
Hide in their bells, a soft aërial blue—

Sweet flowers, that nestle in the humblest nooks,
And yet within whose smallest bud is wrapped
A world of promise ! Still the north wind breathes
His frost, and still the sky sheds snow and sleet ;
Yet ever, when the sun looks forth again,
The flowers smile up to him from their low seats.
 Well hast thou borne the bleak March day of life.
Its storms and its keen winds to thee have been
Most kindly tempered, and through all its gloom
There has been warmth and sunshine in thy heart ;
The griefs of life to thee have been like snows,
That light upon the fields in early spring,
Making them greener.   In its milder hours,
The smile of this pale season, thou hast seen
The glorious bloom of June, and in the note
Of early bird, that comes a messenger
From climes of endless verdure, thou hast heard
The choir that fills the summer woods with song.
 Now be the hours that yet remain to thee
Stormy or sunny, sympathy and love,
That inextinguishably dwell within
Thy heart, shall give a beauty and a light
To the most desolate moments, like the glow
Of a bright fireside in the wildest day ;
And kindly words and offices of good
Shall wait upon thy steps, as thou goest on,
Where God shall lead thee, till thou reach the gates
Of a more genial season, and thy path
Be lost to human eye among the bowers
And living fountains of a brighter land.
 March, 1855.

THE NEW AND THE OLD.

NEW are the leaves on the oaken spray,
 New the blades of the silky grass ;
Flowers, that were buds but yesterday,
 Peep from the ground where'er I pass.

These gay idlers, the butterflies,
  Broke, to-day, from their winter shroud ;
These light airs, that winnow the skies,
  Blow, just born, from the soft, white cloud.

Gushing fresh in the little streams,
  What a prattle the waters make !
Even the sun, with his tender beams,
  Seems as young as the flowers they wake.

Children are wading, with cheerful cries,
  In the shoals of the sparkling brook ;
Laughing maidens, with soft, young eyes,
  Walk or sit in the shady nook.

What am I doing, thus alone,
  In the glory of Nature here,
Silver-haired, like a snow-flake thrown
  On the greens of the springing year ?

Only for brows unploughed by care,
  Eyes that glisten with hope and mirth,
Cheeks unwrinkled, and unblanched hair,
  Shines this holiday of the earth.

Under the grass, with the clammy clay,
  Lie in darkness the last year's flowers,
Born of a light that has passed away,
  Dews long dried and forgotten showers.

"Under the grass is the fitting home,"
  So they whisper, "for such as thou,
When the winter of life is come,
  Chilling the blood, and frosting the brow."

THE TIDES.

The moon is at her full, and, riding high,
  Floods the calm fields with light ;
The airs that hover in the summer-sky
  Are all asleep to-night.

There comes no voice from the great woodlands round
    That murmured all the day ;
Beneath the shadow of their boughs the ground
    Is not more still than they.

But ever heaves and moans the restless Deep ;
    His rising tides I hear,
Afar I see the glimmering billows leap ;
    I see them breaking near.

Each wave springs upward, climbing toward the fair
    Pure light that sits on high—
Springs eagerly, and faintly sinks, to where
    The mother-waters lie.

Upward again it swells ; the moonbeams show
    Again its glimmering crest ;
Again it feels the fatal weight below,
    And sinks, but not to rest.

Again and yet again ; until the Deep
    Recalls his brood of waves ;
And, with a sullen moan, abashed, they creep
    Back to his inner caves.

Brief respite ! they shall rush from that recess
    With noise and tumult soon,
And fling themselves, with unavailing stress,
    Up toward the placid moon.

O restless Sea, that, in thy prison here,
    Dost struggle and complain ;
Through the slow centuries yearning to be near
    To that fair orb in vain ;

The glorious source of light and heat must warm
    Thy billows from on high,
And change them to the cloudy trains that form
    The curtain of the sky.

Then only may they leave the waste of brine
    In which they welter here,
And rise above the hills of earth, and shine
    In a serener sphere.

NOT YET.

Oh country, marvel of the earth!
    Oh realm to sudden greatness grown!
The age that gloried in thy birth,
    Shall it behold thee overthrown?
Shall traitors lay that greatness low?
No, land of Hope and Blessing, No!

And we, who wear thy glorious name,
    Shall we, like cravens, stand apart,
When those whom thou hast trusted aim
    The death-blow at thy generous heart?
Forth goes the battle-cry, and lo!
Hosts rise in harness, shouting, No!

And they who founded, in our land,
    The power that rules from sea to sea,
Bled they in vain, or vainly planned
    To leave their country great and free?
Their sleeping ashes, from below,
Send up the thrilling murmur, No!

Knit they the gentle ties which long
    These sister States were proud to wear,
And forged the kindly links so strong
    For idle hands in sport to tear?
For scornful hands aside to throw?
No, by our fathers' memory, No!

Our humming marts, our iron ways,
    Our wind-tossed woods on mountain-crest,

The hoarse Atlantic, with its bays,
    The calm, broad Ocean of the West,
And Mississippi's torrent-flow,
And loud Niagara, answer, No !

Not yet the hour is nigh when they
    Who deep in Eld's dim twilight sit,
Earth's ancient kings, shall rise and say,
    " Proud country, welcome to the pit !
So soon art thou, like us, brought low ! "
No, sullen group of shadows, No !

For now, behold, the arm that gave
    The victory in our fathers' day,
Strong, as of old, to guard and save—
    That mighty arm which none can stay—
On clouds above and fields below,
    Writes, in men's sight, the answer, No !
July, 1861.

THE CONSTELLATIONS.

O Constellations of the early night,
That sparkled brighter as the twilight died,
And made the darkness glorious ! I have seen
Your rays grow dim upon the horizon's edge,
And sink behind the mountains.   I have seen
The great Orion, with his jewelled belt,
That large-limbed warrior of the skies, go down
Into the gloom.   Beside him sank a crowd
Of shining ones.   I look in vain to find
The group of sister-stars, which mothers love
To show their wondering babes, the gentle Seven.
Along the desert space mine eyes in vain
Seek the resplendent cressets which the Twins
Uplifted in their ever-youthful hands.
The streaming tresses of the Egyptian Queen
Spangle the heavens no more.   The Virgin trails
No more her glittering garments through the blue.

Gone ! all are gone ! and the forsaken Night,
With all her winds, in all her dreary wastes,
Sighs that they shine upon her face no more

Now only here and there a little star
Looks forth alone.   Ah me ! I know them not,
Those dim successors of the numberless host
That filled the heavenly fields, and flung to earth
Their quivering fires.   And now the middle watch
Betwixt the eve and morn is past, and still
The darkness gains upon the sky, and still
It closes round my way.   Shall, then, the Night
Grow starless in her later hours ?   Have these
No train of flaming watchers, that shall mark
Their coming and farewell ?   O Sons of Light !
Have ye then left me ere the dawn of day
To grope along my journey sad and faint ?

Thus I complained, and from the darkness round
A voice replied—was it indeed a voice,
Or seeming accents of a waking dream
Heard by the inner ear ?   But thus it said :
O Traveller of the Night ! thine eyes are dim
With watching ; and the mists, that chill the vale
Down which thy feet are passing, hide from view
The ever-burning stars.   It is thy sight
That is so dark, and not the heavens.   Thine eyes,
Were they but clear, would see a fiery host
Above thee ; Hercules, with flashing mace,
The Lyre with silver chords, the Swan uppoised
On gleaming wings, the Dolphin gliding on
With glistening scales, and that poetic steed,
With beamy mane, whose hoof struck out from earth
The fount of Hippocrene, and many more,
Fair clustered splendors, with whose rays the Night
Shall close her march in glory, ere she yield,
To the young Day, the great earth steeped in dew.

So spake the monitor, and I perceived
How vain were my repinings, and my thought
Went backward to the vanished years and all
The good and great who came and passed with them,   101

And knew that ever would the years to come
Bring with them, in their course, the good and great,
Lights of the world, though, to my clouded sight,
Their rays might seem but dim, or reach me not.

THE THIRD OF NOVEMBER, 1861.

SOFTLY breathes the west-wind beside the ruddy forest,
Taking leaf by leaf from the branches where he flies.
Sweetly streams the sunshine, this third day of November,
Through the golden haze of the quiet autumn skies.

Tenderly the season has spared the grassy meadows,
Spared the petted flowers that the old world gave the new
Spared the autumn-rose and the garden's group of pansies,
Late-blown dandelions and periwinkles blue.

On my cornice linger the ripe black grapes ungathered ;
Children fill the groves with the echoes of their glee,
Gathering tawny chestnuts, and shouting when beside them
Drops the heavy fruit of the tall black-walnut tree.

Glorious are the woods in their latest gold and crimson,
Yet our full-leaved willows are in their freshest green.
Such a kindly autumn, so mercifully dealing
With the growths of summer, I never yet have seen.

Like this kindly season may life's decline come o'er me ;
Past is manhood's summer, the frosty months are here ;
Yet be genial airs and a pleasant sunshine left me,
Leaf, and fruit, and blossom, to mark the closing year !

Dreary is the time when the flowers of earth are withered ;
Dreary is the time when the woodland leaves are cast—
When, upon the hillside, all hardened into iron,
Howling, like a wolf, flies the famished northern blast.

102

Dreary are the years when the eye can look no longer
  With delight on Nature, or hope on human kind ;
Oh, may those that whiten my temples, as they pass me,
  Leave the heart unfrozen, and spare the cheerful mind !

THE POET.

Thou, who wouldst wear the name
  Of poet mid thy brethren of mankind,
And clothe in words of flame
  Thoughts that shall live within the general mind !
Deem not the framing of a deathless lay
The pastime of a drowsy summer day.

But gather all thy powers,
  And wreak them on the verse that thou dost weave,
And in thy lonely hours,
  At silent morning or at wakeful eve,
While the warm current tingles through thy veins
Set forth the burning words in fluent strains.

No smooth array of phrase,
  Artfully sought and ordered though it be,
Which the cold rhymer lays
  Upon his page with languid industry,
Can wake the listless pulse to livelier speed,
Or fill with sudden tears the eyes that read.

The secret wouldst thou know
  To touch the heart or fire the blood at will?
Let thine own eyes o'erflow ;
  Let thy lips quiver with the passionate thrill
Seize the great thought, ere yet its power be past,
And bind, in words, the fleet emotion fast.

Then, should thy verse appear
  Halting and harsh, and all unaptly wrought,

Touch the crude line with fear,
    Save in the moment of impassioned thought ;
Then summon back the original glow, and mend
The strain with rapture that with fire was penned.

Yet let no empty gust
    Of passion find an utterance in thy lay,
A blast that whirls the dust
    Along the howling street and dies away ;
But feelings of calm power and mighty sweep,
Like currents journeying through the windless deep.

Seek'st thou, in living lays,
    To limn the beauty of the earth and sky ?
Before thine inner gaze
    Let all that beauty in clear vision lie ;
Look on it with exceeding love, and write
The words inspired by wonder and delight.

Of tempests wouldst thou sing,
    Or tell of battles—make thyself a part
Of the great tumult ; cling
    To the tossed wreck with terror in thy heart ;
Scale, with the assaulting host, the rampart's height,
And strike and struggle in the thickest fight.

So shalt thou frame a lay
    That haply may endure from age to age,
And they who read shall say :
    " What witchery hangs upon this poet's page !
What art is his the written spells to find
That sway from mood to mood the willing mind ! "

THE RETURN OF THE BIRDS.

I HEAR, from many a little throat,
    A warble interrupted long ;

I hear the robin's flute-like note,
  The bluebird's slenderer song.

Brown meadows and the russet hill,
  Not yet the haunt of grazing herds,
And thickets by the glimmering rill,
  Are all alive with birds.

Oh choir of spring, why come so soon ?
  On leafless grove and herbless lawn
Warm lie the yellow beams of moon ;
  Yet winter is not gone.

For frost shall sheet the pools again ;
  Again the blustering East shall blow—
Whirl a white tempest through the glen,
  And load the pines with snow.

Yet, haply, from the region where,
  Waked by an earlier spring than here,
The blossomed wild-plum scents the air,
  Ye come in haste and fear.

For there is heard the bugle-blast,
  The booming gun, the jarring drum,
And on their chargers, spurring fast,
  Armed warriors go and come.

There mighty hosts have pitched the camp
  In valleys that were yours till then,
And Earth has shuddered to the tramp
  Of half a million men !

In groves where once ye used to sing,
  In orchards where ye had your birth,
A thousand glittering axes swing
  To smite the trees to earth.

Ye love the fields by ploughmen trod ;
  But there, when sprouts the beechen spray

The soldier only breaks the sod
　　To hide the slain away.

Stay, then, beneath our ruder sky ;
　　Heed not the storm-clouds rising black,
Nor yelling winds that with them fly ;
　　Nor let them fright you back,—

Back to the stifling battle-cloud,
　　To burning towns that blot the day,
And trains of mounting dust that shroud
　　The armies on their way.

Stay, for a tint of green shall creep
　　Soon o'er the orchard's grassy floor,
And from its bed the crocus peep
　　Beside the housewife's door.

Here build, and dread no harsher sound,
　　To scare you from the sheltering tree,
Than winds that stir the branches round,
　　And murmur of the bee.

And we will pray that, ere again
　　The flowers of autumn bloom and die,
Our generals and their strong-armed men
　　May lay their weapons by.

Then may ye warble, unafraid,
　　Where hands, that wear the fetter now,
Free as your wings shall ply the spade,
　　And guide the peaceful plough.

Then, as our conquering hosts return,
　　What shouts of jubilee shall break
From placid vale and mountain stern,
　　And shore of mighty lake !

And midland plain and ocean-strand
　　Shall thunder : " Glory to the brave,
Peace to the torn and bleeding land,
　　And freedom to the slave ! "

MY AUTUMN WALK.

On woodlands ruddy with autumn
  The amber sunshine lies;
I look on the beauty round me,
  And tears come into my eyes.

For the wind that sweeps the meadows
  Blows out of the far Southwest,
Where our gallant men are fighting,
  And the gallant dead are at rest.

The golden-rod is leaning,
  And the purple aster waves
In a breeze from the land of battles,
  A breath from the land of graves.

Full fast the leaves are dropping
  Before that wandering breath;
As fast, on the field of battle,
  Our brethren fall in death.

Beautiful over my pathway
  The forest spoils are shed;
They are spotting the grassy hillocks
  With purple and gold and red.

Beautiful is the death-sleep
  Of those who bravely fight
In their country's holy quarrel,
  And perish for the Right.

But who shall comfort the living,
  The light of whose homes is gone:
The bride that, early widowed,
  Lives broken-hearted on;

The matron whose sons are.lying
  In graves on a distant shore;

The maiden, whose promised husband
  Comes back from the war no more ?

I look on the peaceful dwellings
  Whose windows glimmer in sight,
With croft and garden and orchard,
  That bask in the mellow light ;

And I know that, when our couriers
  With news of victory come,
They will bring a bitter message
  Of hopeless grief to some.

Again I turn to the woodlands,
  And shudder as I see
The mock-grape's blood-red banner
  Hung out on the cedar-tree ;

And I think of days of slaughter,
  And the night-sky red with flames,
On the Chattahoochee's meadows,
  And the wasted banks of the James.

Oh, for the fresh spring-season,
  When the groves are in their prime ;
And far away in the future
  Is the frosty autumn-time !

Oh, for that better season,
  When the pride of the foe shall yield,
And the hosts of God and Freedom
  March back from the well-won field ;

And the matron shall clasp her first-born
  With tears of joy and pride ;
And the scarred and war-worn lover
  Shall claim his promised bride !

The leaves are swept from the branches ;
  But the living buds are there,

With folded flower and foliage,
   To sprout in a kinder air.

October, 1864.

THE DEATH OF SLAVERY

O THOU great Wrong, that, through the slow-paced years,
  Didst hold thy millions fettered, and didst wield
  The scourge that drove the laborer to the field,
And turn a stony gaze on human tears,
      Thy cruel reign is o'er ;
      Thy bondmen crouch no more
In terror at the menace of thine eye ;
  For He who marks the bounds of guilty power,
Long-suffering, hath heard the captive's cry,
  And touched his shackles at the appointed hour,
And lo ! they fall, and he whose limbs they galled
Stands in his native manhood, disenthralled.

A shout of joy from the redeemed is sent ;
  Ten thousand hamlets swell the hymn of thanks ;
  Our rivers roll exulting, and their banks
Send up hosannas to the firmament !
      Fields where the bondman's toil
      No more shall trench the soil,
Seem now to bask in a serener day ;
  The meadow-birds sing sweeter, and the airs
Of heaven with more caressing softness play,
  Welcoming man to liberty like theirs.
A glory clothes the land from sea to sea,
For the great land and all its coasts are free.

Within that land wert thou enthroned of late,
  And they by whom the nation's laws were made,
  And they who filled its judgment-seats obeyed
Thy mandate, rigid as the will of Fate.

Fierce men at thy right hand,
With gesture of command,
Gave forth the word that none might dare gainsay ;
And grave and reverend ones, who loved thee not,
Shrank from thy presence, and in blank dismay
Choked down, unuttered, the rebellious thought ;
While meaner cowards, mingling with thy train,
Proved, from the book of God, thy right to reign.

Great as thou wert, and feared from shore to shore,
The wrath of Heaven o'ertook thee in thy pride ;
Thou sitt'st a ghastly shadow ; by thy side
Thy once strong arms hang nerveless evermore.
And they who quailed but now
Before thy lowering brow,
Devote thy memory to scorn and shame,
And scoff at the pale, powerless thing thou art.
And they who ruled in thine imperial name,
Subdued, and standing sullenly apart,
Scowl at the hands that overthrew thy reign,
And shattered at a blow the prisoner's chain.

Well was thy doom deserved ; thou didst not spare
Life's tenderest ties, but cruelly didst part
Husband and wife, and from the mother's heart
Didst wrest her children, deaf to shriek and prayer ;
Thy inner lair became
The haunt of guilty shame ;
Thy lash dropped blood , the murderer, at thy side,
Showed his red hands, nor feared the vengeance due.
Thou didst sow earth with crimes, and, far and wide,
A harvest of uncounted miseries grew,
Until the measure of thy sins at last
Was full, and then the avenging bolt was cast !

Go now, accursed of God, and take thy place
With hateful memories of the elder time,
With many a wasting plague, and nameless crime,
And bloody war that thinned the human race ;

With the Black Death, whose way
Through wailing cities lay,
Worship of Moloch, tyrannies that built
The Pyramids, and cruel creeds that taught
To avenge a fancied guilt by deeper guilt—
Death at the stake to those that held them not.
Lo ! the foul phantoms, silent in the gloom
Of the flown ages, part to yield thee room.

I see the better years that hasten by
Carry thee back into that shadowy past,
Where, in the dusty spaces, void and vast,
The graves of those whom thou hast murdered lie.
The slave-pen, through whose door
Thy victims pass no more,
Is there, and there shall the grim block remain
At which the slave was sold ; while at thy feet
Scourges and engines of restraint and pain
Moulder and rust by thine eternal seat.
There, mid the symbols that proclaim thy crimes,
Dwell thou, a warning to the coming times.

May, 1866.

A BRIGHTER DAY.

FROM THE SPANISH.

Harness the impatient Years,
O Time ! and yoke them to the imperial car ;
For, through a mist of tears,
The brighter day appears,
Whose early blushes tinge the hills afar.

A brighter day for thee,
O realm ! whose glorious fields are spread between
The dark-blue Midland Sea
And that immensity
Of Western waters which once hailed thee queen :

111

The fiery coursers fling
Their necks aloft, and snuff the morning wind,
Till the fleet moments bring
The expected sign to spring
Along their path, and leave these glooms behind.

Yoke them, and yield the reins
To Spain, and lead her to the lofty seat ;
But, ere she mount, the chains
Whose cruel strength constrains
Her limbs must fall in fragments at her feet.

A tyrant brood have wound
About her helpless limbs the steely braid,
And toward a gulf profound
They drag her, gagged and bound,
Down among dead men's bones, and frost and shade.

O Spain ! thou wert of yore
The wonder of the realms ; in prouder years
Thy haughty forehead wore,
What it shall wear no more,
The diadem of both the hemispheres.

To thee the ancient Deep
Revealed his pleasant, undiscovered lands ;
From mines where jewels sleep,
Tilled plain and vine-clad steep,
Earth's richest spoil was offered to thy hands.

Yet thou, when land and sea
Sent thee their tribute with each rolling wave,
And kingdoms crouched to thee,
Wert false to Liberty,
And therefore art thou now a shackled slave.

Wilt thou not, yet again,
Put forth the sleeping strength that in thee lies,
And snap the shameful chain,
And force that tyrant train
To flee before the anger in thine eyes ?

Then shall the harnessed Years
Sweep onward with thee to that glorious height
Which even now appears
Bright through the mist of tears,
The dwelling-place of Liberty and Light.

October, 1867.

————

THE FLOOD OF YEARS.

A MIGHTY Hand, from an exhaustless Urn,
Pours forth the never-ending Flood of Years,
Among the nations. How the rushing waves
Bear all before them ! On their foremost edge,
And there alone, is Life. The Present there
Tosses and foams, and fills the air with roar
Of mingled noises. There are they who toil,
And they who strive, and they who feast, and they
Who hurry to and fro. The sturdy swain—
Woodman and delver with the spade—is there,
And busy artisan beside his bench,
And pallid student with his written roll.
A moment on the mounting billow seen,
The flood sweeps over them and they are gone.
There groups of revellers whose brows are twined
With roses, ride the topmost swell awhile,
And as they raise their flowing cups and touch
The clinking brim to brim, are whirled beneath
The waves and disappear. I hear the jar
Of beaten drums, and thunders that break forth
From cannon, where the advancing billow sends
Up to the sight long files of armèd men,
That hurry to the charge through flame and smoke.
The torrent bears them under, whelmed and hid
Slayer and slain, in heaps of bloody foam.
Down go the steed and rider, the plumed chief
Sinks with his followers ; the head that wears

113

The imperial diadem goes down beside
The felon's with cropped ear and branded cheek.
A funeral-train—the torrent sweeps away
Bearers and bier and mourners.   By the bed
Of one who dies men gather sorrowing,
And women weep aloud ; the flood rolls on ;
The wail is stifled and the sobbing group
Borne under.   Hark to that shrill, sudden shout,
The cry of an applauding multitude,
Swayed by some loud-voiced orator who wields
The living mass as if he were its soul !
The waters choke the shout and all is still.
Lo ! next a kneeling crowd, and one who spreads
The hands in prayer—the engulfing wave o'ertakes
And swallows them and him.   A sculptor wields
The chisel, and the stricken marble grows
To beauty ; at his easel, eager-eyed,
A painter stands, and sunshine at his touch
Gathers upon his canvas, and life glows ;
A poet, as he paces to and fro,
Murmurs his sounding lines.   Awhile they ride
The advancing billow, till its tossing crest
Strikes them and flings them under, while their tasks
Are yet unfinished.   See a mother smile
On her young babe that smiles to her again ;
The torrent wrests it from her arms ; she shrieks
And weeps, and midst her tears is carried down.
A beam like that of moonlight turns the spray
To glistening pearls ; two lovers, hand in hand,
Rise on the billowy swell and fondly look
Into each other's eyes.   The rushing flood
Flings them apart : the youth goes down ; the maid
With hands outstretched in vain, and streaming eyes,
Waits for the next high wave to follow him.
An aged man succeeds ; his bending form
Sinks slowly.   Mingling with the sullen stream
Gleam the white locks, and then are seen no more.

  Lo ! wider grows the stream—a sea-like flood
Saps earth's walled cities ; massive palaces

Crumble before it ; fortresses and towers
Dissolve in the swift waters ; populous realms
Swept by the torrent see their ancient tribes
Engulfed and lost ; their very languages
Stifled, and never to be uttered more.

I pause and turn my eyes, and looking back
Where that tumultuous flood has been, I see
The silent ocean of the Past, a waste
Of waters weltering over graves, its shores
Strewn with the wreck of fleets where mast and hull
Drop away piecemeal ; battlemented walls
Frown idly, green with moss, and temples stand
Unroofed, forsaken by the worshipper.
There lie memorial stones, whence time has gnawed
The graven legends, thrones of kings o'erturned,
The broken altars of forgotten gods,
Foundations of old cities and long streets
Where never fall of human foot is heard,
On all the desolate pavement.   I behold
Dim glimmerings of lost jewels, far within
The sleeping waters, diamond, sardonyx,
Ruby and topaz, pearl and chrysolite,
Once glittering at the banquet on fair brows
That long ago were dust, and all around
Strewn on the surface of that silent sea
Are withering bridal wreaths, and glossy locks
Shorn from dear brows, by loving hands, and scrolls
O'er written, haply with fond words of love
And vows of friendship, and fair pages flung
Fresh from the printer's engine.   There they lie
A moment, and then sink away from sight.

I look, and the quick tears are in my eyes,
For I behold in every one of these
A blighted hope, a separate history
Of human sorrows, telling of dear ties
Suddenly broken, dreams of happiness
Dissolved in air, and happy days too brief
That sorrowfully ended, and I think
How painfully must the poor heart have beat

In bosoms without number, as the blow
Was struck that slew their hope and broke their peace.

Sadly I turn and look before, where yet
The Flood must pass, and I behold a mist
Where swarm dissolving forms, the brood of Hope,
Divinely fair, that rest on banks of flowers,
Or wander among rainbows, fading soon
And reappearing, haply giving place
To forms of grisly aspect such as Fear
Shapes from the idle air—where serpents lift
The head to strike, and skeletons stretch forth
The bony arm in menace.   Further on
A belt of darkness seems to bar the way
Long, low, and distant, where the Life to come
Touches the Life that is.   The Flood of Years
Rolls toward it near and nearer.   It must pass
That dismal barrier.   What is there beyond?
Hear what the wise and good have said.   Beyond
That belt of darkness, still the Years roll on
More gently, but with not less mighty sweep.
They gather up again and softly bear
All the sweet lives that late were overwhelmed
And lost to sight, all that in them was good,
Noble, and truly great, and worthy of love—
The lives of infants and ingenuous youths,
Sages and saintly women who have made
Their households happy ; all are raised and borne
By that great current in its onward sweep,
Wandering and rippling with caressing waves
Around green islands with the breath
Of flowers that never wither.   So they pass
From stage to stage along the shining course
Of that bright river, broadening like a sea.
As its smooth eddies curl along their way
They bring old friends together ; hands are clasped
In joy unspeakable ; the mother's arms
Again are folded round the child she loved
And lost.   Old sorrows are forgotten now,
Or but remembered to make sweet the hour

That overpays them ; wounded hearts that bled
Or broke are healed forever.   In the room
Of this grief-shadowed present, there shall be
A Present in whose reign no grief shall gnaw
The heart, and never shall a tender tie
Be broken ; in whose reign the eternal Change
That waits on growth and action shall proceed
With everlasting Concord hand in hand.

OUR FELLOW-WORSHIPPERS.

THINK not that thou and I
Are here the only worshippers to day,
  Beneath this glorious sky,
Mid the soft airs that o'er the meadows play ;
  These airs, whose breathing stirs
The fresh grass, are our fellow-worshippers.

See, as they pass, they swing
The censers of a thousand flowers that bend
  O'er the young herbs of spring,
And the sweet odors like a prayer ascend,
  While, passing thence, the breeze
Wakes the grave anthem of the forest-trees.

It is as when, of yore,
The Hebrew poet called the mountain-steeps,
  The forests, and the shore
Of ocean, and the mighty mid-sea deeps,
  And stormy wind, to raise
A universal symphony of praise.

For, lo ! the hills around,
Gay in their early green, give silent thanks ;
  And, with a joyous sound,
The streamlet's huddling waters kiss their banks,
  And, from its sunny nooks,
To heaven, with grateful smiles, the valley looks.

The blossomed apple-tree,
Among its flowery tufts, on every spray,
Offers the wandering bee
A fragrant chapel for his matin-lay ;
And a soft bass is heard
From the quick pinions of the humming-bird.

Haply—for who can tell ?—
Aërial beings, from the world unseen,
Haunting the sunny dell,
Or slowly floating o'er the flowery green,
May join our worship here,
With harmonies too fine for mortal ear.

A LEGEND OF THE DELAWARES.

THE air is dark with cloud on cloud,
And, through the leaden-colored mass,
With thunder-crashes quick and loud,
A thousand shafts of lightning pass.

And to and fro they glance and go,
Or, darting downward, smite the ground.
What phantom arms are those that throw
The shower of fiery arrows round ?

A louder crash ! a mighty oak
Is smitten from that stormy sky.
Its stem is shattered by the stroke ;
Around its root the branches lie.

Fresh breathes the wind ; the storm is o'er ;
The piles of mist are swept away ;
And from the open sky, once more,
Streams gloriously the golden day.

A dusky hunter of the wild
  Is passing near, and stops to see
The wreck of splintered branches piled
  About the roots of that huge tree.

Lo, quaintly shaped and fairly strung,
  Wrought by what hand he cannot know,
On that drenched pile of boughs, among
  The splinters, lies a polished bow.

He lifts it up ; the drops that hang
  On the smooth surface glide away :
He tries the string, no sharper twang
  Was ever heard on battle-day.

Homeward Onetho bears the prize :
  Who meets him as he turns to go ?
An aged chief, with quick, keen eyes,
  And bending frame, and locks of snow.

" See, what I bring, my father, see
  This goodly bow which I have found
Beneath a thunder-riven tree,
  Dropped with the lightning to the ground."

" Beware, my son ; it is not well "—
  The white-haired chieftain makes reply—
" That we who in the forest dwell
  Should wield the weapons of the sky.

" Lay back that weapon in its place ;
  Let those who bore it bear it still,
Lest thou displease the ghostly race
  That float in mist from hill to hill."

" My father, I will only try
  How well it sends a shaft, and then,
Be sure, this goodly bow shall lie
  Among the splintered boughs again."

So to the hunting-ground he hies,
　To chase till eve the forest-game,
And not a single arrow flies,
　From that good bow, with erring aim.

And then he deems that they, who swim
　In trains of cloud the middle air,
Perchance had kindly thoughts of him
　And dropped the bow for him to bear.

He bears it from that day, and soon
　Becomes the mark of every eye,
And wins renown with every moon
　That fills its circle in the sky.

None strike so surely in the chase ;
　None bring such trophies from the fight ;
And, at the council-fire, his place
　Is with the wise and men of might.

And far across the land is spread,
　Among the hunter tribes, his fame ;
Men name the bowyer-chief with dread
　Whose arrows never miss their aim.

See next his broad-roofed cabin rise
　On a smooth river's pleasant side,
And she who has the brightest eyes
　Of all the tribe becomes his bride.

A year has passed ; the forest sleeps
　In early autumn's sultry glow ;
Onetho, on the mountain-steeps,
　Is hunting with that trusty bow.

But they, who by the river dwell,
　See the dim vapors thickening o'er
Long mountain-range and severing dell,
　And hear the thunder's sullen roar.

Still darker grows the spreading cloud
  From which the booming thunders sound,
And stoops and hangs a shadowy shroud
  Above Onetho's hunting-ground.

Then they who, from the river-vale,
  Are gazing on the distant storm,
See in the mists that ride the gale
  Dim shadows of the human form—

Tall warriors, plumed, with streaming hair
  And lifted arms that bear the bow,
And send athwart the murky air
  The arrowy lightnings to and fro.

Loud is the tumult of an hour—
  Crash of torn boughs and howl of blast,
And thunder-peal and pelting shower,
  And then the storm is overpast.

Where is Onetho? what delays
  His coming? why should he remain
Among the plashy woodland ways,
  Swoln brooks and boughs that drip with rain?

He comes not, and the younger men
  Go forth to search the forest round.
They track him to a mountain-glen,
  And find him lifeless on the ground.

The goodly bow that was his pride
  Is gone, but there the arrows lie ;
And now they know the death he died,
  Slain by the lightnings of the sky.

They bear him thence in awe and fear
  Back to the vale with stealthy tread ;
There silently, from far and near,
  The warriors gather round the dead.

But in their homes the women bide ;
   Unseen they sit and weep apart,
And, in her bower, Onetho's bride
   Is sobbing with a broken heart.

They lay in earth their bowyer-chief,
   And at his side their hands bestow
His dreaded battle-axe and sheaf
   Of arrows, but without a bow.

"Too soon he died ; it is not well"—
   The old men murmured, standing nigh—
"That we, who in the forest dwell,
   Should wield the weapons of the sky."

BIOGRAPHICAL

SOURCES

A PARTIAL LISTING

William Cullen Bryant: The Prose Writing, Russell and Russell, Inc., 1964, New York.
The Letters of William Cullen Bryant, Volumes I and II, edited by William Cullen Bryant II and Thomas G. Voss, Fordham University Press, New York, 1975 and 1977.
The Poetical Works of William Cullen Bryant, Henry C. Sturges, with Memoir by Richard Henry Stoddard, The Roslyn Edition, AMS Press, New York, 1903, 1972.
William Cullen Bryant: English Men of Letters Series, William Aspinwall Bradley, Mac-Millen Co., London-New York, 1905, Edited by Charles Warner.
Three Voices From Paumanok, Joan D. Berbrich, Ira J. Friedman Inc., Port Washington, N.Y., 1967.

William Cullen Bryant, John Bigelow, Houghton, Mifflin and Co., The Riverside Press, Cambridge, 1890.

William Cullen Bryant, Charles H. Brown, Charles Scribner's Sons, New York, 1971.

The Century Association's Memorial Statue of William Cullen Bryant: Report of the Memorial Committee, no date, no publisher.

Literary Characteristics of Democratic Times, A. DeToqueville.

The Early History of Roslyn Harbor, Conrad Godwin Goddard, Printed by the Author.

A Biography of William Cullen Bryant with Extracts from His Private Correspondence, 2 volumes, 1883, reprinted 1967, both New York. by Parke Godwin.

Politics and a Bellyful: The Journalistic Career of William Cullen Bryant, Civil War Editor of the New York Evening Post, Curtiss S. Johnson, Greenwood Press Publishers, Westport, Connecticut, 1974.

A New Library of Poetry and Song, Edited by William Cullen Bryant, J. B. Ford Company, 1877, New York.

Poems of William Cullen Bryant, Humphrey Milford, Oxford University Press, London-Edinburgh, Glasgow, New York, Toronto, 1914.

William Cullen Bryant, Representative Selections, with Introduction, Bibliography and Notes, Tremaine McDowell, University of Minnesota American Book Co., 1935.

Liberals Among the Orthodox, Unitarian Beginnings in New York City, 1819–39, Walter Donald Kring, Beacon Press, Boston, 1974.

Gotham Yankee, Harry Houston Peckham, Vantage Press, 1950.

American Literature, Poets of National Culture to 1830, Revised Edition, Edited by Robert E. Spillen, Harold Blodgett, New York, The MacMillen Company, New York, 1949.

Literature in America, Philip Rahv, Meridian Books, New York, 1957.

Adventures in American Literature, Schweikert, Anglis, Gehlmann, Foerster, Harcourt Brace and Company, New York and Chicago, 1938.

Literary Haunts and Homes: American Authors, Theodore F. Wolfe, J. B. Lippincott Company, 1898.

Long Island As America: A Documentary History to 1896, Edited by James E. Bunce and Richard P. Hammond, National University Publications, Kennikat Press, Port Washington, New York-London, 1977.

History of Long Island, From Its First Settlement by Europeans to the Year 18 (*date obscure*), Nathaniel S. Prime, published by Robert Carter, New York, 1845.

American Agitators and Pen Portraits of Living American Reformers, David Bartlett, Miller, Orton and Mulligan, Auburn, New York, 1855.

History of Long Island, Benjamin F. Thompson, E. French, publisher, New York, 1839.

The Evening Post: A Century of Journalism, by Allan Nevins, Boni and Liveright, N.Y., 1922.

Collections:

New York Public Library:
    Bryant-Godwin Collection
    Goddard-Roslyn Collection
    William Cullen Bryant-Miscellaneous
Bryant Library, Roslyn, New York

East Hampton Library
    Long Island Collection

Manuscripts:
Unpublished Letters of William Cullen Bryant: Edited by Helen L. Drew.
Notes From the Leggett Diary: Bryant Library, Roslyn, New York.
William Cullen Bryant and Isaac Henderson, New Evidence on a Strange Partnership, Theodore Hornberger, University of Tennessee Press.

Magazines, Newspapers
Munsey's Magazine
Illustrated Family Newspapers
Brooklyn Eagle
Harper's New Monthly Magazine
New York Evening Post

INDEX

126

The Bryant Photo Album

Bryant in 1843, just one year
before the New York Evening
Post editor became the owner of
a forty-acre estate in Roslyn
that he named Cedarmere. In
photo at right is his wife,
Frances Fairchild, as a young
woman, from a miniature
on ivory painted by
an unidentified artist.

Frances (Fanny) Bryant,
eldest daughter of William
Cullen and Frances Bryant,
shown as a young woman
in the early portrait (above)
and as a married woman
(Mrs. Parke Godwin) in the
Dresden miniature (below)
painted in Europe.

Julia, the Bryants' youngest daughter, is shown left in photograph on the lawn at Cedarmere. Below, Julia in later years. She never married, was her father's frequent traveling companion after her mother's death. It was Julia who carried out her father's wishes and established what was to become the Bryant Library in Roslyn, after his death in 1878.

Miniature of Mrs. Bryant, in her
later years, was painted by
Günther Friedrich Reibic of
Dresden, from a photograph
by C. R. Fredreck. Mr. Bryant
commissioned the miniature
after his wife's death.

Bryant in 1825, when
he came to N.Y.
as literary editor . . .

And in 1843,
just before he bought
his country place . . .

. . . In 1869, after he'd
become a prestigious
force in public life . . .

. . . And in later, waning
years, when he translated
Homer, while still editing
the N.Y. Evening Post.

Photo at top shows Bryant's writing
desk, with one of his European travel
journals. Miniature desk sat on one knee
when he wanted to write during travel.
Desk legs folded for easy storage.
Another of his journals, and one of his
wife's, are shown along with
a copy of one of a series of health
tracts called "The Health Habits of
William Cullen Bryant and
William Howitt."

This was brought to me by James Arlington Bennett who had a herald's office in New York, as the coat of arms belonging to the Bryant family. The wreath — a laurel wreath he called it — he admitted, was an addition of his own.
W. C. Bryant
Roslyn Sept 1854.

Coat of arms of the Bryant family was
brought to Bryant by James Arlington
Bennett, who had a herald's office in New
York City. Bryant's handwritten note, which
was dated September 1854, says Bennett
admitted that the laurel wreath
was an addition of his own.

Shown are "The
Roslyn Edition" of the author's
translations of Homer, and a
small edition of one of his
poems, "The Unknown Way."

"The Bryant Birthday Book," with
appropriate quotes for each day
taken from his works. Note the
open pages for a February day.
All Bryant's works were printed
in the ornate style of his
century, with gilt edges and
elegant calligraphy. Form and
style in publishing were always
important to the poet-editor.

A bucolic view of Hempstead Harbor, as rural as Roslyn still was when Bryant first visited.

This Bufford lithograph shows Cedarmere as residence of Joseph Moulton, from whom Bryant bought it in 1843.

A13

The grounds of Cedarmere, with
artificial lake in foreground, and
Bryant's greenhouses at right, are
depicted in photo post-card.

Stereopticon views, in succession,
of the bridge and small pond below
the main house at Cedarmere.
Card is part of a series from
the estate of the poet.

View often drawn and painted of Cedarmere. Julia's boathouse can be seen on the shore of the lake.

Gardens Bryant developed with the aid of George Cline, his gardener-manager in 1860's. Photo was taken in early 1900's.

A16

Family photo at Cedarmere, shows Julia at right with dog and Bryant at left. The others are family members and friends.

Black walnut tree on Bryant's estate
was the oldest, and biggest, on
Long Island. The tree lived for
143 years. Visitors to Bryant's
home often were made impromptu
gifts of handsful of the tree's fruit.

One of many cottages Bryant built
on his estate for his family and
friends was Sweetbriar. Original
house had board and batten
sheathing, with scalloped trim.

Goldenrod was the cottage Bryant
had built—between pond and
shore—for his daughter Fanny
and her husband, Parke Godwin,
sometime between 1843 and 1845.
Godwins' daughter Minna was born there.

Stone House on the estate was begun by
George Cline, Bryant's manager, around
1866. It wasn't completed until about 1872.
House is still in use today and despite
additions and changes, resembles the
original structure.

Montrose, one of the buildings already
existing on the estate when Bryant enlarged his
holdings, had been built in 1834 by William Hicks.
Later it was enlarged for Bryant's daughter
and son-in-law, Fanny and Parke Godwin.

The poet in his later years, depicted at work
in his library at Cedarmere, where he
translated the works of Homer.

Another view of the poet's home in Roslyn,
in an early lithograph. The fireplace in the
drawing room was lined with ceramic tiles.

A familiar scene to Bryant might have been the sight of schooner "Highlander," with Captain Peter Lynch at wheel. It is shown docking at old Hicks Lumberyard, then behind Roslyn mill. It made regular trips to Albany for bricks and to Maine for lumber. Date of photo is approximately 1865.

This photo shows a steamboat docking at Emory's Landing near the foot of Bryant's Cedarmere. In good weather, Bryant took a paddle-wheel steamer to and between home in Roslyn and office in Manhattan.

The steamboat that ran from Oyster Bay to New York City. Picture was taken from the dock at Glenwood Landing.

The paper mill in Roslyn Park was one of the largest in
New York State when Bryant was a resident. Water
from the (present) Roslyn duck pond supplied the power,
flowing through the water wheel to the harbor. Replica of
mill building is still in the park, though unused.

The Roslyn depot of the Long Island Railroad wasn't built until
1887, nine years after Bryant's death. But he wouldn't have
been surprised to see the buggy—since it was a
common way to travel in the days when he went to Mineola
depot by stage coach to take the railroad to Manhattan.

Silver Lake still came up to the edge of Old Northern Boulevard in Bryant's time, as it did in this photo, taken in 1888. Dating is possible because of kerosene lamps and telephone wires.

In Bryant's day, Old Northern Boulevard was a toll road with two toll booths, one located in what is now Roslyn Cemetery, where the poet is buried.

In this lithograph, circa 1836, Cedarmere, then known as Springbank can be seen in foreground. Ships that plied the harbor took commuters to Manhattan from the dock (at center right) in about three hours in good weather.

The steam-engined train that Bryant characterized in one letter as "that sooty suburban train" is shown at the Roslyn depot. For some of the years that Bryant commuted there were no trains to Roslyn. He went by stage to Mineola, where he boarded the train for Brooklyn. From Brooklyn he took a ferry to his Manhattan office.

The Hall, donated by Bryant in his will to the community where he'd spent 35 years. It was established as a library and a meeting place for villagers, because Bryant was concerned that the only meeting places in the village were numerous bars.

A27

By 1885, Bryant's son-in-law, Parke Godwin, who also was
Bryant's first biographer, was the president of the
Bryant Circulating Library Association. This share, at
$5, was sold to Walter Hicks.

In that same year, Robert Hicks purchased
a membership in the Bryant Circulating
Library Association, for the sum of one dollar.

In 1890, the Roslyn community paid tribute to the
library's founder with presentation of a memorial
plaque at a special program.

PROGRAMME OF EXERCISES

——) AND (——

PRESENTATION OF MEMORIAL TABLET,

IN HONOR OF WILLIAM CULLEN BRYANT,

At Bryant Hall, Monday, November 3d, 1890.

(Anniversary of the Birth of the Poet.)

Singing by pupils of Roslyn Public School.

(Hymn by William Cullen Bryant)

Mighty One, before whose face
  Wisdom had her glorious seat;
When the orbs that people space
  Sprang to birth beneath Thy feet.

Source of truth, whose beams alone
  Light the mighty world of mind;
God of love, who from Thy throne
  Kindly watchest all mankind.

Shed on those, who, in Thy name,
  Teach the way of truth and right,
Shed that love's undying flame,
  Shed that wisdom's guiding light.

Presentation of Tablet and acceptance by Trustees.

Singing by children.

(Hymn by William Cullen Bryant.)

As shadows cast by cloud and sun
  Flit o'er the summer grass,
Lo, in Thy sight, Almighty One,
  Earth's generations pass.

And so the years and endless host
  Come swiftly pressing on;
The brightest names that earth can boast,
  Just glisten and are gone.

Yet doth the Star of Bethlehem shed
  A luster pure and sweet,
And still it leads as once it led
  To the Messiah's feet.

Oh, Father, may that holy star
  Grow every year more bright,
And send its glorious beams afar,
  To fill the world with light.

Roslyn News Job Print.

The "Programme of Exercises and Presentation of Memorial Tablet" in the poet's honor included the singing of a hymn Bryant had written. Pupils of the Roslyn Public School were members of the chorus at the celebration, held in honor of Bryant's birthday.

A31

Photographic portrait shows
Bryant in the later years of his life.

PHOTO CREDITS

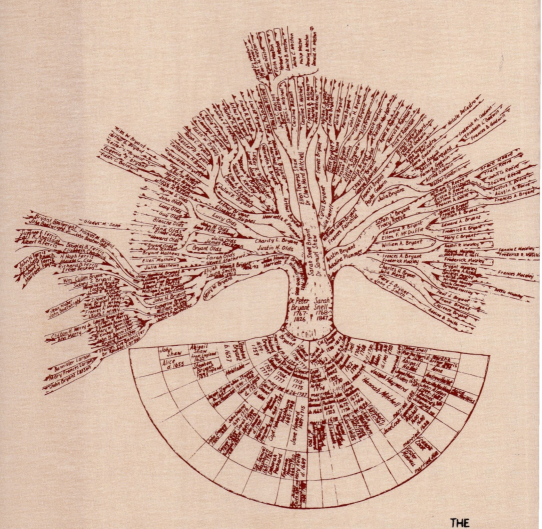

THE

BRYANT FAMILY

Compiled and Arranged
by
Lester C. Bryant
Princeton Ill. July 1974